MY FUNNY SEX STORIES

A HYSTERICAL COLLECTION OF A PRO ATHLETE'S SEXCAPADES

By

WES DAVIDSON

Beezy Publishers

Published in the United States of America.
First Edition 2013
Beezy Publishers
Pittsburgh, PA 15237
www.beezypublishers.com
www.myfunnysexstories.com

ISBN: 978-0-9889675-1-9
EISBN: 978-0-9889675-0-2

Library of Congress Control Number: 2013932735

Cover design by Tim Pryor
Interior Design by Ramesh Kumar Pitchai
Beezy Publishers logo by Sean Easter

To all the condom manufactures,
for building something that helped keep me safe
and warm and my willy wet.

To all the women mentioned in this book,
thank you for allowing me to bestow this dick upon thee.

Table of Contents

Introduction

How is your sex life? Normal? Healthy? Wild? Dead and needs to be revived? Unborn? Whatever your situation is, I consider mine extravagant, rare, and maybe even sometimes dangerous. But the best adjective to describe my sex life? Comical. And primary the contributing factor to my interesting sex life is sports.

I've been fortunate enough to play sports at a professional level for (insert # of years). Playing in the big leagues is a dream I've had ever since I knew how to throw a ball. And once I got there, I wanted to live that life up as best I could. I didn't do drugs. I didn't drink much alcohol. But I DID do the women. And (un?)fortunately, that habit stuck with me like my shadow.

This book will explain and describe this habit that has gotten me into some unique situations; it is a book based on my sex life, or "sexcapades". As a former athlete, model, and actor, the pussy-cat has always purred at me. I have visited countless cities across the globe and found enough women to have multiple sequels to Moulin Rouge. But the point is not the quantity of women, but the quality (or, in some cases, the lack thereof) of the women. It is the most awkward situations that turn into the best stories for friends.

Like many of you, I use my friends as personal, free shrinks. What's the point in paying someone all that money to listen to you when your friends will do it for some high fives and maybe a

7

milkshake?! My friends and I are able to sit down usually a restaurant, and have open conversations about personal problems, reminisce about past events, and discuss future plans. And of course, we talk about romantic relationships.

One day, my friend and I decided to have lunch at a fast food spot. While my buddy was in the middle of devouring his burger and fries, I was telling him about how I somehow managed to sleep with a married woman…whose husband just so happened to be a CIA agent (I told you that my sexcapades can be dangerous!). After illustrating the drama that went down in that whole debacle, my friend pushed me to write about my sexual escapades. This book contains that story, along with many more that will have you either laughing, shaking your head, or questioning how in the world one man can get himself in the ridiculous situations I've been in.

These stories were inspired by my popular website, www. myfunnysexstories.com. A majority of the names in this book have been changed in order to protect the dignity of those involved. If you are a girl I have hooked up with and one of these stories sounds all too familiar, keep on reading because I'm sure that there is another story in there that will make you think, "at least I wasn't THAT girl!"

For everyone else: These are true stories. *My stories. My sex stories. My Funny Sex Stories.*

Chapter 1

The Triple Play

When you turn on ESPN, it is commonplace to see a double play occur during the highlights. Rarely will you see a triple play during a round of SportsCenter. If you do, it will definitely make SportsCenter's Top 10 Plays of the Week. A triple play occurs when a team makes three outs in one play thus ending the inning. However, in the world of women, a triple play occurs when you knock down three women in the same inning (24 hours). I have committed many triple plays in my lifetime, and each one was an experience. However, on this particular triple play, I was able accomplish it in three different cities.

Join me as I share with you one of my triple play stories, from the first to the third out. It is near the holidays, and I had recently lost my passport. I am supposed to be flying from LA to Spain in a week to visit this girl I had been banging off and on for the past four years. I had to expedite a replacement passport in order to get onto the plane. The passport agency tells me that I need to be in line at the LA federal building at 8 AM on Friday. I decide to bring some excitement to this week from all the stress of getting a new passport.

First Out

It's five o'clock Thursday morning, in smog filled LA, and I wake up next to this girl Maria I just bumped and grinded R. Kelly style all night. Maria had begged me to give it to her the previous day because her man was on a road trip. He was a forward for the sorry-ass LA Clippers, and she was looking for a new rebounder for her team. While she laid there passed out, I rolled over to check my cell phone, which had been on silent all night. Damn, ten missed phone calls and five voicemails from my girl Gabby, in San Diego. I walk out to Maria's living room and listen to the 5 messages.

MESSAGE 1: *Hey, was calling to see how your day was! I love you and miss you, muah!*

MESSAGE 2: *Hi, babe it's me just wanted to see if you were still coming over tonight to watch some TV, and I cooked your favorite lasagna.*

MESSAGE 3: *This is the fifth time I'm calling tonight...where are you?*

MESSAGE 4: *OK. Obviously you have seen me call a ton of times. So I take it that you are mad at me. If it's something that I did, please tell me, and I promise to fix it. I just want you to be happy.*

MESSAGE 5: *Now, I am worried. The food is cold, I wanted to make tonight special and I even lit candles at the dinner table.*

Just text me back or something so that I know you are ok. Its two AM *and I still have not heard from you since I got off of work. I am working from home tomorrow so call me it does not matter what time. I just want to know you are ok.*

One thing I can't stand is a desperate woman. Some women don't have common sense. *Why do you think I'm not answering the phone?* It is not because I was just kidnapped by Sasquatch. Don't you know if I'm not answering my phone, I'm doing one of two things: 1) Fucking or 2) Trying to fuck future pussy after just fucking some present pussy. I call her back, and she answers the phone half a sleep. I talk in my sleepy raspy voice, "Hey, I had fallen asleep, and my phone was on silent. I just was calling to let you know that I am OK." She could barely make out what I was saying and mumbled a few words before the conversation was over and she hung up the phone.

As I walk back to the bedroom, Maria's alarm clock starts going off. It's time for her to get up for work. She is laying there topless in a red thong as the sunlight starts to peek through the blinds. Then, the thought came to me: *I can commit a double play today.* She gets up and goes to the bathroom to brushes her teeth. As she is intensely brushing her teeth, I stand in the bathroom doorway watching her double D titties sway from left to right and right to left as if they were trying to hypnotize me. Maria had a body that every woman envied and every man lusted over. She was the kind of woman that you wanted to walk around with in public because people would shake their heads in disbelieve that you were fucking such a bad bitch.

She then walks in to the kitchen to make me some scrambled eggs and toast. I grab her hips from behind if we were starting to

salsa dance.   She slides her thong off, and I start rubbing her clit from behind. I frisk her naked body like a police officer looking for contraband. She starts moaning, and I enter the penis parking lot. While I have her bent over on the kitchen counter, I notice her tramp stamp.

Viva la Vida

"*Long live life.*" I had seen this tramp stamp before, but this was the first time I actually reading it. It gives me motivation for the day and I decide that today, I am going to "live life". Cognizant of the fact that she had to be at work this morning, I treat our sex session like a sprint rather than a marathon. I was more like Usian Bolt than Lance Armstrong. It was just *wham, bam, mamacita, thank you, senorita.*

She finished cooking breakfast while I run to the bathroom to flush the condom down the toilet and wash my nuts. I get dressed and grab a plate to go. With breakfast in hand, I head out the door like a first grader on his first day of school. I jump in my car and drive over to the gas station to fill up the car. While I'm there I think about Maria and her NBA player's relationship. One thing I have learned about professional athletes is they have women in every city. However, those women have other men. Sometimes those men are the athlete's agents, their teammates, or just random guys that can blow their back out better than they can. Relationships are just a game. The individual with the best defense and offense is the one that wins. Those that are not built for this game end up getting heartbroken.

With a full tank of gas, I am now ready to "live life," like Maria's tattoo says. I can sense that this is going to be an interesting day. I start the car up and head down to San Diego to see my Italian girl.

I could use the two-hour drive, because it affords me a rest from all the fucking I have been doing. Over the years I have realized that most Italian girls are nymphomaniacs, and my girl was no different. They love two things: 1) sex and 2) cooking. Some of their sex drives are so high even I have trouble keeping up with them. When messing with an Italian girl, you'd better come with your A-game. Otherwise, you could be in danger of getting a BDR (Bad Dick Report), which basically translates to: *you suck in bed.*

An hour and half into my drive to San Diego, I get a "Good morning" text from Erica. Erica is this half black, half white girl that I know in Phoenix and we had been talking over the phone the past few months. I met Erica at one of my friend's weddings in Colorado Springs over the summer. She was in her last year of law school at Arizona State. Law School has a way of robbing people from their social life. Law students are either at home, in class or in the library. The thing I love about women in law school is that they get right to the point when it comes to sex. They don't have time to cuddle after sex because they need to get back to the books. I don't have time to cuddle because my services are needed in other places.

Erica loved to send me naked pictures to my phone. I guess she had no other life outside law school, and I provided an outlet for her. We have never had sex before, but she was like a bitch in heat begging for every dog in the neighborhood to quench her thirst. As I drive, our text message exchange goes something like this:

Me: *Hey, sexy, good to hear from you. What r u up to?*
Erica: *Just thinking about u.*
Me: *Oh really? What r u thinking about?*

ERICA: *To be honest, I just got done masturbating and
imagining that you were inside of me*
ME: *So when r we going to make your fantasy a reality?*
ERICA: *Whenever you are ready but you live all the way in
Cali.*

I am very spontaneous when it comes to women. As I continued to
drive, I could not stop thinking about Maria's tattoo. *Live life.* I knew
that I had to be back in LA at 8:00 AM but I said. "What the hell."

ME: *What are you doing tonight?*
ERICA: *I am doing the finishing touches on this paper. Y?*
ME: *Cause I'm coming over. Send me your address*
ERICA: *Yeah right. Don't tease me like that*
ME: *I will come but the only thing is that I have to be in LA in
the morning so I can't stay long but I want to see you.*

Erica sends me a text with her address. I smile, because I have a
chance to make a triple play. Not only are they hard to come by,
but if I complete the triple play, I will have knocked the bottom out
of three different girls separated by a total of 848 miles: 120 miles
from LA to San Diego, 355 miles from San Diego to Phoenix, and
373 miles from Phoenix to LA. Three major cities, three beautiful women with three different ethnicities. I basically was having
Enchiladas (Maria) for breakfast, Spaghetti (Gabby) for lunch, and
Fried Chicken/Apple Pie (Erica) for dinner. I let Erica know that I
will be in Phoenix by midnight. My dick is like the former FedEx
slogan: *When it absolutely, positively has to be there overnight,* it's *not
just a package,* **it's your business.**

Second Out

I finally arrive in San Diego to Gabby's house around noon. I am starving from all the calories I burned while in LA. Sex cardio will get the fattest man in shape quickly. Have you ever seen a fat player? *Exactly.* Players never get fat because they are constantly having sex.

Gabby has a hot plate of leftover Lasagna on the table for me and I scarf it down while she massages my shoulders. She then lets me know that she is going to finish up one of her work assignments. Gabby was a top executive at a prestigious accounting firm and had a really nice place on the beach. While she finishes her work, I decide to take the opportunity to lie down and rest up for my next workout.

I was awakened out of my deep sleep by Gabby trying to speak into my microphone. I look up at her, my vision still blurry from my nap, just in time to see her start to bounce on my dick like kid who has just discovered how to ride a pogo stick. She cums faster than Charlie Sheen can say *winning* after doing a line of coke. Gabby has a special superhero-type of power when she cums. She would squirt all over the bed. Half of the time, when getting ready to bump uglies with her, I didn't know whether to put my swimming goggles on or call a lifeguard. She squirted so much during sex that we eventually had to invest in a plastic mattress cover to prevent her from ruining the mattress.

As I start to wake up to this pussy squirting everywhere like a malfunctioning sprinkler system, I flip her over and do my best rendition of Rin Tin Tin and hit it doggy style. It was like a game of copycat. She fucks me, I fuck back. I fuck harder; she fucks harder. She talks

shit, and I feel like the shit. Then we are like two singers harmonizing during a duet. She is singing soprano, and I'm singing tenor. We are saying the same thing. She sings her best rendition of "I'm cuming," and I follow suit.

Now, the grand finale. We both orgasm at the same time like we had been rehearsing it for years. I am now covered in pussy juice and sweat. The sweat came from the hard work and the pussy juice came from working it hard. I glance over at the clock on her dresser. It reads 5:50 pm. *Shit, I have to be in Phoenix in a few hours.*

I jump up to take a shower and she grabs my arm. "Where are you going, babe? Keep giving it to me!" I have already busted three nuts today. Two in LA and one in San Diego. Like a cowboy who is down to his last bullet in the chamber, I weigh my options on how I am going to shoot this last bullet. I can spend the next hours trying to cum again for Gabby or I can take a five-hour intermission and dip my stick into new pussy that was manufactured in Phoenix. I decide on the latter.

I explain to Gabby that I have to go to the bathroom real quick so I can change out my condom. While in the bathroom, I run the water so that Gabby can't hear me from the other room. I call my friend Todd. Todd picks up.

ME: "Hey."
TODD: "Whats up man?"
ME: "Can you hear me?"
TODD: "Yeah, but why are you whispering?"
ME: "I need you to do me a favor. It's 6:00; call me in exactly two minutes."
TODD: "Umm…OK."

I hang up the phone turn my ringer from silent to loud and leave it in the bathroom while walking back to the bedroom with my dick in my hand. We start kissing and getting things started again. Just like clockwork, Todd calls my phone. I leap up and rush to the phone.

"Are you really leaving me to answer the phone? Tell them you will call them back later!" Gabby demands. I ignore her request and pick up the phone. Then, I walk back into the bedroom with the phone attached to my ear.

TODD: "Hey, you wanted me to call you..."

ME: "Yeah what's up?"

TODD: "That's what I am trying to figure out. You asked me to call you!"

ME: "Oh really? Oh my goodness, are you OK?"

TODD: "Uh, why would I not be OK?"

ME: "OK, let me think."

TODD: "Think about what? You are not making any sense right now."

ME: "Alright, what freeway did you say that was?"

TODD: "Are you drunk right now? Are you even talking to me?"

ME: "Okay, I will be over there to pick you up. Just be patient and wait for me."

TODD: "Dude, I'm a little concerned about you. What's going…"

I hang up on Todd. Worried, Gabby asks if everything is okay. I tell her that Todd's car has broken down on the freeway and he does not have AAA so I have to go get him. I escape the nympho's

house by the skin of my teeth. I jump back in my car and call Todd to explain what was going on. I am now on the Interstate 8 freeway headed to Phoenix. An hour into my drive, I call Gabby and let her know that I got Todd and that everything was Okay. I also tell her that I will be spending the night with Todd, because heneeds a ride to work in the morning.

Third Out

I arrive in Phoenix a little after midnight. I knock on Erica's door and she answers the door in the sexiest black Fredrick Hollywood lingerie I have ever seen. Her titties were pushed up and perky, almost as if they were saluting me. All of her lights were turned out in the apartment and she had candles lit everywhere throughout apartment.

> ERICA: "You must be hungry from that long drive. I made some chicken casserole if you are still hungry."
> ME: "I would love some, but can I use your shower? I have been in the car for five hours straight."
> ERICA: "Sure. The towels and washcloths are in the cabinet down the hall right before you reach the bathroom."

I hop in the shower and get myself clean. When I get out of the shower, I don't even bother putting all my clothes on. I sit at the table and eat the chicken casserole in nothing but my boxers. Out of the corner of my eye, I can see Erica checking out my body. Hitting her velvet lined meat wallet was going to be easy. This ham was cooked glazed and ready to be sliced. After finishing the plate, I throw it in the sink.

ERICA: "Don't you think that you need to get a little rest?
I'm glad you came out here to see me. What time do you
have to be in LA again?"
ME: "8:00 AM."
ERICA: "Wow, I think we should lie in the bed so you can
get some rest."

I had already anticipated me not getting any rest. I even stocked up
on a few red bulls for the road trip on the way back to LA. Erica and I
lay in bed, and she goes in for the kill. She immediately starts rubbing
my cock. We start sucking face and next thing I know, I am putting
Mr. Johnson in the sperm jacuzzi. I lay the pipe like I have something
to prove. Since I am such a competitor, when her girlfriends ask
her who the best person she has slept with, I want her to think of
me. Our sex session is like my golf game. I'm using a high number
of strokes for various holes while using my club on manicured grass.

I finish getting it on with Erica and glance over at her clock. It
reads 3:00 am. I spring up out of the bed and throw on my clothes; I
throw my shirt on then I try to put my pants on while simultaneously
running out the door. I can't be late to my appointment in LA. Erica is looking at me and shaking her head at my clumsiness. She sums
up the night pretty well by saying, "It is a shame what men will do
for pussy." And with those words of wisdom, I head back to the LA.

I jump on the 10 freeway headed west while looking at the
city of Phoenix in my rear view mirror. I can't believe what I had
just done. I did the unthinkable, got credit for the rare triple play
while visiting three different cities. I spent a significant amount of
money on gas but it was worth every cent. I guess it pays to have
fun. *Vive la Vida.* But more importantly, *Vive la Triple play.*

Chapter 2

A Baby D.A.D.D.Y. Drama

This story is about a D.A.D.D.Y. (Dangerous Angry Deranged Dad, You're fucked) and dedicated to all the men who have ever dated a woman with a child.

It is 1:30 pm, and I am driving around looking to grab a bite to eat. After eating in a shopping center, I decide to randomly catch a drama movie playing at 2:15 pm. While standing in line to get pop-corn topped with that mystery substance they claim to be butter, a cougar behind me in line me taps me on the shoulder.

COUGAR: "Excuse me, can I ask you a question?"
ME: "Sure."
COUGAR: "Are you single?"

Me, in my smoothest mack daddy voice "Yes, I am single."

COUGAR: "Well that is good. And why don't you have a girlfriend? You're really hot!"

At this point I am smiling while sizing this cougar up. She is half White and half Korean. Just like exotic pets and cars, I love exotic women. Not a lot of people have them so when you get them,

people love to stare. I notice this exotic cougar is wearing a wedding ring with a diamond the size of a small rock. I figure this woman must be a freak, because she is sporting a huge wedding ring and asking me if I am single. Let's play ball, because I have my bat and balls ready to swing one into her catcher's mitt. One thing I like about cougars is they know what they want and pounce on it. I guess that is why they call them cougars. No strings attached, just straight wild animal sex. However, my assumptions about this cougar's intentions prove to be wrong.

I bait her for some sympathy in hopes that she will pounce on me:

ME: "Well I just got out of a relationship not too long ago. I am looking for that special someone in my life to ease my fears. That is why this hot guy is at the movies all alone by himself. Would you like to join me? I need an attractive woman by my side such as yourself."

COUGAR: "Haha. You are pretty bold. I like it, though! Unfortunately, I am married, but I wanted to connect you with my cousin. It's a good thing you are outgoing because she is extremely shy. She really thinks you're attractive and so do I. She is standing right over there. She is too shy to come up to you. So that is why I tapped you on the shoulder."

She points across the room. Sure enough, I see this younger woman in her early 20's standing there acting like she is not paying attention to what had just transpired. I could tell this woman was very shy, but she was so attractive that it made up for any character flaw she

currently had. It was something I could work with. She was such an introvert; it was like she was afraid to make eye contact in my direction. The cougar's cousin was half Black and half Korean. She resembled the R&B singer from the early 2000's, Amerie.

After paying for the popcorn, I write my phone number on a napkin. I walk over to greet the shy, sexy Blasian (black and Asian). I attempt to throw her a funny line in order to break the ice and get the panties moist like Duncan Hines.

ME: "Hello, my name is Wes."
BLASIAN: "Hi, I'm Charity."
ME: "Well, Charity it is a pleasure meeting you. I was just talking to your cousin. I see attractiveness runs in your family."
CHARITY: "Why, thank you."
ME: "You're quite welcome. I'm sorry but I have to cut this conversation short, because my movie is about to start. However, here is a napkin. When you open the napkin, you will see ten numbers. The numbers are a combination. When you open your cell phone, type in that combination. As you enter more and more numbers to that ten-digit combination on your cell phone, the closer you will get to me. Just think of it like ten degrees of separation."

She laughs hysterically.

CHARITY: "That was a good one! Well, enjoy your movie..."

Mission accomplished. I just threw her a line; she bit. I'm willing to bet she needs to make a pit stop in ladies room, because her panties are soaked from her Blasian pussy juice. I head towards my movie, with my popcorn in one hand and a potential tray of Blasain ass on a platter in the other.

Two and half weeks later, I am sitting on my couch watching the evening news. At this point, I had forgotten about meeting Charity at the movies. My cell phone rings, and it is a call from a number I don't recognize.

ME: "Hello."
CHARITY: "Hi...is...this...Wes?"
ME: "It depends on who is asking."
CHARITY: "This is Charity."
ME: "Charity? As in Jerry's Kids?"

She laughs. Another point added to the coochie coupon that I plan on redeeming in the near future.

CHARITY: "No, not sure if you remember me. I met you
at the movie theaters and you gave me your number.
Sorry it took so long for me to call. I was going through
some personal issues, but I am okay now."

When a woman tells you that you she couldn't call you, because she was going through some personal issues, you know this is a red flag! Sadly though, I am addicted to pretty woman with nice asses, and it often clouds my judgment.

ME: "Umm, ok. Normally my number has an expiration date if I don't hear from people in a week. Since, this one is for Charity; I am going to let it."

Charity laughs and we spent the next fifteen minutes on the phone getting to know each other. During the next few days while talking on the phone with her, she reveals that she has a 6 year old son. I usually don't date women with crumb snatchers (kids). The reason for this is because I will never be a priority to that woman and will always come second to her kid. On the other side, I would never want a woman that puts me over her kid either. Trying to date a woman with kids is the ultimate catch 22. Charity was no different, but I was determined to get a slice of her poontang pie.

After dating Charity for a few months and getting plenty slices of the poontang pie, she invites me over to her second story apartment one day. I arrive at her apartment and she is visibly upset. Her eyes were red and she had the meanest snot stache.

ME: "What's wrong?"
CHARITY: "It's my baby's father. I really don't want to talk about it."
ME: "You can tell me. You are not going to me something that I have not heard before."
CHARITY: "He was just saying really mean things to me."

Me: "Just randomly? You must have done something to piss him off. People just don't randomly say mean things unless they have a reason."

CHARITY: "You don't know my ex."

ME: "I don't know your ex, but I know people."
CHARITY: "Trust me...he is crazy!"

I am in complete disbelief. Every bitter single mom blames everything on their ex. These moms act like it is the man's fault for depositing semen in their penalty boxes. News flash: *It takes two to tango.* As far as I am concerned, Charity is probably still seeing her ex and they are fighting over some relationship bullshit.

> **ME:** "I refuse to believe that he is just goes off on you for nothing. You don't have to explain yourself cause it's none of my business. I know if it was me, I would not take that stuff from him. You are a grown ass woman. When he calls you, and it is not about your son, then you don't need to be on the phone with him."

Just as I tell her this, her cell phone rings. It happens to be her ex. She answers the phone and he is yelling out her so loud that I hear his voice from where I am standing. She pulls the phone away from her mouth, covers up the receiver, and leans over and whispers to me, "See, he is yelling at me again!"   She then hands me the phone so I can hear.

Sure enough, I hear a male's voice on the other line, "...And that is why you are a dumb bitch. You fucking hoe. You ain't shit bitch. I wish I never got you pregnant in the first place, because my son's mother doesn't know shit..."

I hand the phone back to a timid Charity. Then, like a supportive Pep rally, I root for team Charity. Charity remains on the phone with the angry black man and I whisper in her ear instigating the argument.

ME: "Don't take the shit from him. Remember, you're a grown woman. He is telling you what is on his mind. Tell that greedy bastard what's on your mind! Give him a taste of his own medicine...see how he likes it!"

Charity gains an immediate rise in her confidence level and nods her head in agreement.

CHARITY: "No, I'm not going to shut up. Why don't you shut up! I don't have to take your shit. Oh...oh...fuck me? No, fuck you. You can kiss my ass, Marlon! I was afraid to stand up to you before, but I'm not afraid of you anymore."

Each statement that Charity makes to Marlon becomes bolder and bolder while standing up for herself. In between statements, I give her high fives and fist pumps as if I am at a European soccer game. She then reaches the highest level of boldness by telling him that he can suck a dick and hangs up on him.

My jaw drops. I look as if I am in the blue corner and my fighter just KO'd the champ. I am proud of her because this shy introvert just stood up to the man who had been verbally abusing her for years. No wonder she is so shy and insecure. This man had been spitting venomous darts to her self-esteem for a long time. The bully finally met his match.

Like a team that has won the championship, I suggest that we go eat lunch to celebrate. Charity, her crumb snatcher, Albert, and I, decide on *PF Changs*. It is not Korean food, but it is a close second. While eating, we have a brief conversation about her ex.

ME: "So, now, I believe you. Your ex is crazy."

CHARITY: "See, what did I tell you? I know what I am talking about. I have been dealing with him for years. It's like he gets in these crazy moods. He is not on drugs or anything; he is just crazy."

ME: "Oh I see. He is not crazy enough to come to your house, is he?"

CHARITY: "No, I don't think he is that crazy. He usually cools down after awhile. Besides, he lives two hours away in LA. I am really glad you told me to stand up to him. I feel so much better. He just does not want me to be happy. The good thing is that I have been happy ever since I met you at that movie theater."

ME: "Does he know about me?"

CHARITY: "No, I have not told him anything. He can just tell that I am a lot happier for whatever reason."

She thanks me again for coaching her through the phone conversation. She then reaches over, grabs my crotch and lets me know that she is going to thank me in other ways when we get back to her apartment.

When we arrive back at her place, little Albert starts to get sleepy. She puts on some cartoons for him to watch in the living room. He starts to get so sleepy that his head begins to swivel like a wet noodle. His eyes keep rolling back in the back of his head until he can longer fight it. He finally crashes on the couch.

Charity and I hurry to the bedroom like it is an all you can eat Chinese buffet. We lock the bedroom door and I take off her panties to expose her fortune cookie. She grabs my California roll and

begs for my Beijing Beef. I reach for her fortune cookie which feels like it was drenched in some egg drop soup. Things start to get wasabi hot. I'm ready to fill her wonton with cream cheese and we begin stir-frying. I go Kung Pao with my beef in her broccoli. She calls me her General Tso while I am deep in her moo shu. She starts begging for me to spill my duck sauce all on her fried rice. Like Lui Kang from Mortal Kombat, I use my own finishing move. I pull my chopstick out of her rice bowl and sprinkle soy sauce all over her back. With her back now looking like the aftermath of a Chinese New Year, she goes to the shower to wash up.

I pass out as if I had spent the whole day drinking Sake. Only I am pussy drunk. A little while later and still hung-over from pussy, I am awoken by a loud voice. Still discombobulated, I turn to my right and see a naked Charity passed out next to me. I hear the voice again. This time I have identified the where-abouts of this voice and recognize it as a male's voice. It is coming from outside the bedroom window. It sounds as though someone is calling for their lost dog. This time I make out the dog's name. I hear it a third time: *ALLLLLLLbert!*

I conclude that someone has lost a dog named Albert. I roll over and try to go back to sleep. The voice gets louder. *Albert!*

This time, I hear a response and it is far from a dog's bark. It comes from the next room and it sounds like a child's voice, *Daddy!*

Charity all of sudden springs out of the bed like a jack in the box. She goes to the nearby window and looks out of the window.

CHARITY: "Oh my goodness, oh my goodness."
ME: "What's wrong?"
CHARITY: "My ex, Marlon, is outside the fucking window!"

Houston, we have a problem. I realize that voice number two is Albert in the next room. Albert had been woken up from his nap by his angry father outside just like I had. Charity rushes to throw her clothes on and runs to the living room where Albert is. She tries to quiet him down but he refuses. Albert continues to call the five-letter word that still haunts me today from this incident. D.A.D.D.Y.

MARLON: "I am coming up there, son!"

Charity is freaking out. She then discloses to me that Marlon carries a gun in his car and hides it in his glove box. She says that he is not afraid to use it. I hear this DADDY marching up the stairs toward Charity's front door. I am contemplating jumping out of the window because a broken leg is better than losing my life. He starts banging on the door like he is the police.

MARLON: "Open this mutha fuckin' door so I can see my son! Charity? I know you are in there. Why are you not opening this door? Oh I see how it is. You MUST have another nigga in there! Whose dick are you sucking? You wanna be all bold on the mutha fuckin' phone and tell me to suck a dick? I got something for you suck on bitch!"

I think I need to change my pants. I tell Charity to call 911. I tell her again. I am praying that the San Diego police department gets to her apartment before two bodies have to be carried out in body bags. Marlon is still in the background, yelling for Charity to open the door. Every second that goes by seems like a year.

MARLON: "I know one thing; you better NOT have no nigga around my kid. I know that. I will come up and shoot every mutha fucka in there. You don't want to open the door? If my son was not in there, then I would shoot this mutha fuckin' door down....Albert?"

ALBERT: "Yes"

CHARITY: "Shhh. Be quiet son."

ALBERT: "But I want to talk to Daddy!"

MARLON: "Albert...listen to me son. What is the man's name that is in there with you?"

I look at Albert, sweating profusely while shaking my head *no*. Albert looks back at me like he feels sorry for me but is obligated to follow his father's orders.

ALBERT: "Wes!"

MARLON: "See, bitch, I knew you had a mutha fucka around my kid. I told you about that, now both of you got to pay. That is how it's going to be. Mutha fuckas want to play with my life and carrying on. You two can't hide in that apartment forever. I will be waiting right outside for my son. Soon as I get my son, that's yo' ass Charity and that nigga Wes. I got something for ya'll..."

Marlon walks back down the stairs to his car, which is parked across the street. I am shook. In the famous words of Outkast, *the situation is looking bad and I need hope like the words maybe, if or probably.* **Maybe...** the police will get here before I get shot. *If...*

I had stuck to my own advice regarding dating women with kids, I **probably** wouldn't be in this situation.

I start to have a mini debate with myself in my head. *I never thought I would say this but I think I am going to die. Well... no. I don't think I am going to die. I think I can talk my way out of this one. I'll be fine. No wait...This crazy guy just drove two hours down the freeway because his baby momma hung up on him and he just found out another guy is in the apartment with his 6 year old son. Yeah... I'm going to die.*

At this point, I can see Marlon's car from Charity's window and he is just sitting in there. The windows to his car are tinted, so I have no idea what is going on in there. He leaves for a bit and then comes back and parks the car in the same spot. Charity is still on the phone with the 911 operator. Albert is trying to look out of the window to see where his daddy is. As for me, I know *if* and *when* I make it out of this apartment, I will no longer be participating in Chinese Buffet sex with Charity. I will be doing my best impersonation of Clark Gable and be *Gone with the Wind*.

Charity is now crying, because she is so scared. She starts blaming me for Marlon's tirade. She starts claiming that if it weren't for me encouraging her while on the phone with him, he would have never came down from LA. Then, like a President Obama announcement that Osama Bin Laden has been killed; I get breaking news. The police have arrived.

The officers pull up and surround Marlon's car with their guns drawn. They slowly approach his vehicle while he simultaneously gets out of his car with his hands in the air. The police put him in handcuffs and sit him on the sidewalk as they search his car for weapons. In the meantime, another officer comes to the door and takes a statement from Charity and I. Come to find out, she

already had a restraining order against Marlon earlier that year, but it had expired.

After our statements are made, I look in the distance and see the police instructing Marlon to leave. Apparently, the police could not find the gun and had to let him go. FML.

As the sun was setting on a beautiful southern California day, I give Charity a hug and tell her I was on my way home. I had no plans on coming back and seeing Charity ever again. It was fun while it lasted until the day I met a D.A.D.D.Y. This was too much for me. I was thankful I made it out alive. I was free at last, free at last and so glad Marlon didn't kill my ass. Coincidentally, when I met Charity, I was at the movie theater to see a drama flick. My story with Charity ended the same way it started: with a whole lot of drama. Only this drama had a D.A.D.D.Y. playing one of the main characters and I almost lost my life. Cheers: to every man that has had to deal with a baby mother and a D.A.D.D.Y. but was fortunate enough to live and tell the story.

Chapter 3

Alone on the Couch

he unexpected things that can happen while sitting on your couch....alone.

I'm living in LA at the time, and I'm alone on my couch waiting on this fat girl, Naomi, to come over and blow me to sleep. Fat girls are like brussel sprouts; you will try them if they happen to be on your plate, but they are nothing you would brag to your friends about. She was the type I would call over when I was too lazy to jack off. She had a real pretty face and big tits, but her self-esteem was lower than a snake's belly. While Naomi is in route, my wild and crazy cousin, Shawn from Compton, calls me.

SHAWN: "What's going on? How about you come out with your cousin for the evening. I have not seen you in awhile and we need to catch up."

ME: "I can't tonight; I got something coming through in a minute."

SHAWN: "Man, tell that ho, you will be with her another night. Tell her that you have to spend some time with your cousin."

ME: "What's the catch? I know you just don't call me unless you have something up your sleeve."

SHAWN: "No it's nothing. I just want to hangout with my cousin. OK, truth be told...this girl, Keri, I have been talking to, just bought a new bed and wants me to come put it together. The only thing is she lives all the way out in Rancho Cucamonga, but she has a fine ass roommate. You should try and get on her but I think she has a man."
ME: "I knew it. It has been a minute since we hung out. Let me call this girl back. I'll be over there to pick you up in a minute."

When most people hear Rancho Cucamonga they think that it is some mystical place but it is an actual city about forty miles east of LA. They say, *a bird in the hand is better than two in the bush*, so I'm debating on whether to cancel plans with Naomi or try my luck with Shawn. The only thing better than pussy is new pussy. The difficult part is getting new pussy when you have guaranteed pussy. This night I was feeling risky so I told Naomi that my cousin broke down on the 10 freeway, and I had to go get him. She understood and even offered her services when I got back later that night. I pick up my cousin in Compton and we head towards Rancho.

At this point, I could care less about what happens with the females because it just felt good to hang out with my cousin on a mini road trip. On the way to their house, my cousin tells me how bad he wants to fuck Keri's roommate but it would never happen because they are close friends. He is hoping that I can meet her and eventually fuck so that he can live vicariously through me.

When we get to the house Shawn introduces me to his girl, Keri, and her roommate, Jasmine. Shawn and I then go to Keri's room and set up the new bed. While putting the bed together,

she keeps us company by telling us how she can't wait to start her MBA program in the fall at UCLA. She is one of the most intelligent, gorgeous, and down to earth black women I have seen. She is on the skinny side with huge tits.

On the other hand, her roommate Jasmine is eating a fruit salad in the kitchen. Jasmine is a fine ass dark skinned Jamaican. She has long natural wavy hair and an ass that goes on for days. She is also a nurse at the local hospital. After we put the bed together we all go back to the kitchen were Jasmine is. Jasmine is sipping on some wine and getting a little tipsy. There are no stats to prove this theory, but I believe wine alone can increase your chances of getting in a woman's pants by twenty-five percent. Keri asks Jasmine if there is any more wine left and grabs a glass.

After about an hour chit-chatting about nothing, Shawn suggest that we all play a game of truth or dare to spice up the night. I had never really played the game but had heard about it. I thought it was a dumb game the college students played when they had nothing better to do. The first couple rounds are boring, and sure enough, I'm regretting the decision to come all the way out here. I could have been getting brain from Naomi right now. The four of us are only asking general truthquestions. Throughout the game I can tell that Jasmine is giving me the "eye" and there is some sort of mutual attraction going on.

Shawn decides to spice the game up, and when it's Keri's turn, he dares her to go in her room put on her sexiest lingerie, and wear it for the rest of the game. Sure enough, she goes to her room and comes back out in the sexiest lingerie she had in her repertoire which displays her out of this world body. I'm trying not to look at her, because I don't want to disrespect Shawn. Now

that we are getting more daring. It's my turn and Jasmine dares me to strip down naked and pose for five minutes like I'm a playgirl model. I am now seeing daylight in this once boring game of truth or dare. Sure enough, I strip down, and I'm chilling with my meat hanging out.

My cousin goes in the next room so he doesn't have to witness this foolishness. I catch both girls meat-watching and trying to size me up. The liquor is working, and I can sense these girls are starting to get hornier. Like a shark that can smell a drop of blood a mile away in the ocean, men can sense when a bitch's pussy is starting to get wet. I throw my boxers back on and call my cousin back in the room.

It is now Jasmine's turn:

ME: "Truth or Dare?"
JASMINE: "Truth."

At this point I just go out on a limb. You don't win in Vegas if you don't take a risk once in awhile.

ME: "Do you want to fuck me right now? I'm not saying you would, I'm just asking if that thought has crossed your mind."
JASMINE: "Uh...well...umm....yeah it has crossed my mind."

My cousin and I smile at each other, and we know there is a strong possibility the night is about to change fast for the better. I know how he thinks and his next chess move changes the whole mood for the night. With Shawn you always have to expect the unexpected. It's Keri's turn.

SHAWN: "Truth or Dare?"

KERI: "Dare."

SHAWN: "I dare you to kiss Wes."

KERI: "What did you just say?"

ME: "Yeah, what did you just say?"

SHAWN: "You heard what I said. It's just a game, right? Ya'll are acting all scared. Keri, you have to kiss Wes. It can't be no peck; it has to be a kiss for two minutes, and I want to see tongue."

KERI: "Ok, but I'm only doing this because I love you."

Keri walks over to me and tongues me down with a side order of passion. Our mouths are in a wrestling match; hers on top of mine, mine on top of hers. Shawn and Jasmine set down their drinks and are clapping and cheering during the whole two minutes as though they are witnessing an encore performance by the New York Symphony. Shawn and I are like partners in a spades game; we are feeding off each ready to trump this whole game.

It is Shawn's turn.

JASMINE: "Truth or Dare?"

SHAWN: "Dare."

JASMINE: "I dare you to strip down to your boxers."

SHAWN: "Aww…that ain't shit."

Shawn strips down to his boxers and waits for his next turn. I understand where this game of truth or dare (aka spades) is going, and I can't leave my partner out to dry.

It's Jasmine's turn.

ME: "Truth or Dare?"
JASMINE: "Dare."
ME: "I dare you to get naked...in the shower, with Shawn."

She hesitates and looks at Keri for approval. Keri shrugs her shoulders and next thing I know, they both take off their clothes and heading towards Keri's room to the shower. Keri and I are still sitting in the kitchen, and we can hear Shawn and Jasmine giggling. There is one thing about a jealous woman; she will do anything if it means competing with another woman. Keri right now is pissed, because her fine ass roommate is having fun with her man and both are naked.

KERI: "Fuck this fuckin' game."

She then commands me like an army general.

KERI: "Take off your clothes; we are going in there!"

Like an honorable soldier, I follow the general's orders. We both get naked, and I'm all excited to go to war. She holds my hand and leads the way to battle. I now have my gun cocked, loaded, and ready to shoot. Right when we turn the corner, Shawn is already feeling her titties, as if he is prepping her for a mammogram. At this point, there are four adults the shower. I am closest to the shower head; right behind me is Keri. Then, Jasmine, and Shawn is in the very back. I start to feel hands feeling on my chest, and I look over my shoulder, and it's Keri smiling at me.

Her hands move down to my gun and she starts giving me a hand job. I return the favor by flicking her bean as if I am trying to

tune an old guitar string. I'm moving my finger back and forth, forth and back, along her clit. She is getting wetter by the second. Then, all of a sudden, she kind of pushes me away. She is getting jealous that her Shawn and Jasmine are now making out behind us in the shower. She pulls Jasmine off of Shawn and switches places with her. My dick is now hard as a rock, and Jasmine looks down at it.

It was an awkward moment so I look down at it as well and jokingly say, "It's not going to suck itself"

Jasmine surprisingly agrees with my statement. "You are absolutely right."

She gets on her knees and starts licking my dick like a kid on welfare who has just bought her first popsicle from the ice cream man. It was as if was she wanted to prove that she was a member of the all-blow job team three years in a row. She was definitely proving it. She was going to work like a world-class boxer just bobbin and weavin. Keri and Shawn stopped whatever they were doing and gave their best impression of a scene in Friday.

"Daaaaaaaaaaaaammmmnnn." I was about to bust on everyone in the shower, so I had to stop Jasmine from her masterpiece of a blowjob and instruct her to bring this out to the living room.

I throw her on the couch and start blowing her brains out missionary style. She starts screaming and it's turning on the other couple that is still in the shower. They come out to the living room to see what all the commotion is. Shawn figures this is his only chance to get it in with Jasmine so he runs over to the couch where I'm blowing her brains out and sticks his dick in her mouth. Shawn has now just ruined my stroke all because he wanted to get greedy. This scene is not going over well with Keri. She pulls me out of the pussy and begs me to start fucking her like I was doing

her roommate. I'm feeling kind of charitable at the moment so I leave one pussy only to enter into another piece of pussy. Meanwhile, Jasmine can't really talk because Shawn's dick is down her throat, and she is still displaying her all-blow job team skills.

Keri is bent over on all fours in the middle of the living room. I approach the pussy as if I am Peyton Manning approaching the line of scrimmage while yelling audibles. Only my dick is under the center. I enter and she is loving it. Jasmine looks over and is sees that I am fucking the shit out of her roommate. So she pops the dick out her mouth comes and lies in front of us. Keri now bends over a little further and starts eating out Jasmine. I can't believe what is happening right now. I am pounding the shit out of Shawn's girl while she is licking Jasmine's pussy. Shawn is baffled at the whole scene so he pulls Jasmine away from us and is now next to me and he is fucking Jasmine missionary style. We look like two chariot racers from the Roman Empire on the track.

Keri starts to have an orgasm and starts calling out my name "Oh, Wes, fuck me harder...you're giving it to me so good. Oh, Wes."

Shawn stops fucking Jasmine and gives Keri a puzzled look.

SHAWN: "What the fuck? You just called out his name? You don't even say my name when I'm fucking you."
KERI: "You know I didn't mean anything by it. Anyway, you have nerve. You are fucking my roommate right now!"
SHAWN: "Yeah well we are going to have to talk about this later...."

Keri gets up and goes to talk to Shawn. I start fucking Jasmine while Shawn and Keri start to argue. I make Jasmine cum. She is now satis-

fied and wants to return the favor. I'm feeling like a major league baseball player, because I just made a double play; two bitches just came in the same inning. Jasmine and I move away from the argument in the living room, and I bring my bat and balls to the dining room. She sits in a chair at the dining room table, and she goes to town on my bat finishing off what she had started in the shower. She sucks faster and faster; then, I explode all over her face and neck like a chemistry experiment gone wrong. She screams and runs to the bathroom since she failed to put on goggles for this chemistry experiment, and her eyes are burning like disco inferno.

Jasmine is now in the bathroom washing up; Shawn and Keri are still in an argument because Keri said my name. Keri is fed up and storms to her room and slams the door behind her. "I'm going the fuck to bed!"

Jasmine walks out of the bathroom and sees me and Shawn standing there. "Where is Keri?"

Shawn lies and says, "She had a stomachache and went to bed, but we still have work to do."

Shawn takes Jasmine to her bedroom. I am left all alone in the living room. I go and knock on Keri's bedroom. I then hear a voice from inside Keri's room. "Leave me the fuck alone!"

I go back to the crime scene, throw on my clothes and lay on the couch and start thinking to myself. I can't believe how everything went down tonight. I started out calling a fat bitch over, canceling plans with her, driving forty miles to help construct a bed which subsequently led to me banging two girls via a game of truth or dare. I laugh, shake my head in disbelief and wonder how comfortable Keri's new bed is feeling. The night has now ended just like it started. Alone on a couch.

Chapter 4

The Day My Gun Malfunctioned

am in LA for the summer and decide to stay with one of my closest friends, Ray. Ray is living in a one-bedroom apartment in Torrance, CA. Ray had a stable of actresses, models, and other "Hollywood" hopefuls in his repertoire that would often visit. Ray was not a player, not a pimp, but somewhere in between. This one model he was dating, Daphne, would actually give his crazy ass her Mercedes during the week to drive around. Ray would tell her that his car was always in the shop and he needed her car.

She would give him the keys when she was doing photo shoots. He would drop Daphne off at work then pick me up so we could go to the Beverly Center and get a few numbers from the LA women. The bad thing about having Daphne's car during the week is that Ray had to return it once the weekend arrived. That meant we would have to roll in Ray's car. Ray's car was an old model Geo Metro that he randomly bought off of Craigslist for a meager five hundred dollars. My laptop computer back then was worth more than his car.

This Geo Metro was both Geo and Metro. It was Geo because we could probably drive from the west coast to the east coast and back on a quarter tank of gas. This car was a Hybrid before there were Hybrids. It was Metro because it was a Metro-sexual hide-

ous green. This car was a compact car in the most literal sense. It was like taking a yoga class every time you got in it or had to get out of it. You had to bend your body in ways you never expected. Once you were in it, there was nowhere to hide from public ridicule. People at the bus stop would laugh and point and us as we drove around LA. There were no tinted windows and I don't think it went over 40mph going downhill. Sometimes, when we would park this car, the steering wheel would even lock on its own. It was like the car came equipped with an invisible "club". We would sit there for hours hoping that it would unlock by itself. Although the steering wheel would lock, Ray never had any other problems with the car. The Geo Metro was like the ugly girl's number in your phone; she got the job done when you needed her to but you were reluctant to take her out in public.

Ray and I would dress up in nice suits, jump in the Metro and head to the infamous Century Club. Let me retract that statement. We would head *towards* the Century Club. When Ray and I would get within a quarter mile radius of the Century Club, we would start looking for parking. I swear, every time we found a parking space we heard the theme song for mission impossible. Upon parking, we would look around like two paranoid crack heads. We would look over our shoulders to the left and the right to make sure nobody saw us getting out of the car. We would then make our quarter mile journey to the club in our dress shoes. Once we got in the club, the women would flock to us. We came to the realization very quickly that women love men in suits. They never saw the car we drove; they only assumed we drove something nice because of what we wore to the club. Since the majority of club

goers were not wearing suits, we stood out and women always thought we had to be important people.

One night, when Ray and I are in the Century Club, I meet this Egyptian girl from Anaheim. Her name was Rene. She was caramel, completed with the most beautiful hazel eyes I had ever seen. It happened to be her 21st Birthday that night. I saw her on the dance floor, dancing with some her friends trying her best not to spill the drink in her hand. With my back turned to her I purposely backed up into her.

ME: "I am so sorry! I didn't even see you back there."

Rene turns and smiles at me.

RENE: "It's OK."
ME: "I was going to say something to you just now, but you're so pretty that I forgot my pick up line."

Rene laughs.

RENE: "Well, I guess you're going to have to remember if you want to talk to me."
ME: "I'll make a deal with you. Give me your number and I will call you once I remember the pickup line. If you don't answer, when I call then I will leave a message and leave the pickup line on your voicemail. If you like it, call me back. If not I will never call you again. How does that sound?"
RENE: "You have a deal."

Rene gives me her math, and I called a few days later. I made up some cheesy pick up line when I finally called and it worked. Sure enough she called back and we began dating. I was not sure if it was the cheesy pickup line or she was already interested in me. Maybe a little bit of both. Her parents were stricter than a juvenile drill sergeant. She had a curfew every day of the week and had to check in, ever so often, over the phone.

Renee happened to be a virgin, and I was on a mission to be the first in her stadium. Rene worked at the front counter of the Marriott hotel and I figured this was a great thing, because I could stay in the hotel, and she could come see me on her lunch breaks. I rented a room at the Marriott a few times in hopes of popping her cherry, but the mission failed every time. We would only get so far when hooking up. When I would get to the point of trying to slide her panties down, she would stop me every time like a traffic light in downtown. Finally, I got sick of wasting my money on rooms at the Marriott and just gave up trying to put my dong in her hamper of goodies.

Whenever she got off of work, she could barely spend any time with me in the hotel room because her parents were expecting her home right away. She would frequently lie and tell her parents the reason for her tardiness was because she had to stop for gas on the way home. It felt like she was on house arrest.

Weeks went by and Renee was denying me left and right, whenever I would try and snatch the penis purse. I knew that there was a zero chance of me getting her goodies. Not only was she a 21-year old virgin, but her parents were making her check in every hour on the hour. This was probably the most difficult time I had ever had in trying to sleep with a girl. I was jumping through

hoops. I was getting to the point to where she was just not worth pursuing anymore. Then one day she calls me like a representative from the Publishing House Sweepstakes:

ME: "Hello?"

RENEE: "Are you ready to have sex with me?"

ME: "Huh? Can I get a hello from you before you start asking me questions you know you wouldn't do?"

RENE: "Do you or don't you?"

ME: "Uh...yeah sure. Where is this coming from all of a sudden?"

RENE: "It's my parents. They're too strict on me, and I'm sick of it. They don't want me drinking; they don't want me having sex; they just don't want me living. I am freak- ing 21 years old. So are you in or not?"

ME: "Well, I'm not **IN** it right now but hopefully will be in the near future. But on a serious note, I think you should really think about this."

RENE: "I have. I want it to be you. I'm not going to be a virgin forever so I might as well get it out of the way now."

ME: "Yeah, you do have a point. Some man is going to take your virginity; it might as well be me."

RENE: "OK. Did you want to get a hotel room tomorrow?"

ME: "No, I'm not going through that again. How about this, I will get back you later on tonight."

RENE: "OK."

I hang up the phone, and I can't believe what I am hearing. I dial Ray right away on the phone and tell him the good news. Ray lets me

use his one bedroom apartment in order to get down with the get down. The only problem with Ray's apartment is that the a/c is out of order for the week and maintenance is currently trying to get it fixed. This creates a problem for me because in times of extreme heat, I am like an engine that has overheated; none of my pistons fire correctly and I can't get started up, if you know what I mean. I text Rene and tell her to meet me at Ray's house around 9:00 p.m. She willfully agrees and lets me know that she has a midnight curfew.

I arrive early at Ray's house the following day around 7:00 pm in order to get the room right for the next female that will be increasing my batting percentage. Sure enough, the living room is hot like a dick sucker's breath in the morning. In order to take precautionary measures and make the bedroom cooler; Ray allows me to strategically place some of the fans from the living room into the bedroom. Once I get the bedroom down to a decent temperature, I go back to the living room with Ray. Ray then equips me with some of the most valuable weapons for any Casanova: 1) his last condom and 2) the remote to his stereo.

Just as Ray hands me my two weapons, I get a text from Renee letting me know that she is downstairs and needs to be let in. Ray and I then come up with a quick game plan. He tells me that he is going to run to the store so she thinks nobody else is in the apartment. That way, it will help ease any type of butterflies she has in her stomach. Also, it will give me enough time so that I can get her in the room and turn the music on. By that time he will be able to come back in the apartment and watch TV without her hearing him.

I go let her in the front gate as Ray sneaks out of the back. I open the apartment door and we head straight for the bedroom.

Soon as we get into the bedroom, the room is flooded with the sounds of the classic CD I had put on in anticipation for this monumental event. I had put on the Cool Relax CD by Jon B. That album tends to hypnotize a woman into dropping her panties to the floor.

Next, I make her comfortable by rubbing her back and shoulders. Then, we start having small talk about her day. After that, she starts kissing me on my neck. I don't know if Ray was trying to pull a prank on me or not but the temperature started getting really hot all of a sudden. I start sweating, partly because I am a little nervous, and because it felt like a hot humid summer in Houston.

Trying my best to ignore the summer temperature in the room, our tongues start to wrestle like a WWE match. My tongue on top of her tongue, her tongue moving for position trying to body slam mine. We simultaneously start taking each other's clothes off.

As we rumble and tumble naked in the bed with Jon B in the background she whispers in my ear, "I'm ready for you to be inside of me. Do you have a condom?" Without hesitation I reach for the jimmy hat on the dresser. By now the CD is on track 7 *Are you still down featuring Tupac.* I put the condom on, and I am ready for game time.

With her legs spread apart, I am lined up in the backfield, ready to hit the hole like a running back in a college bowl game. However, the temperature in the room started to feel like it had just raised another thousand degrees. The thermostat felt like it went from 100 degree Houston hot to 1,000 degree Gonorrhea hot. By now, sweat is running down from my forehead to my eyes to the point that it's hard for me to even see.

With my dick in my hand I approach the pussy like a 747 Jet on the runway. To my surprise, as I reach for my final destination, my ding a ling loses its ding. Panicked, I try to shake it like a Polaroid picture in order to revive it back to life. "This can't be happening to me right now!" I tell myself. Again, I try to get my pecker back up. Ironically, I hear Jon B over the radio "How does it feel to be useless?" An eager Rene starts to get impatient.

RENE: "Is everything OK?"
ME: "Yeah, everything is fine."
RENE: "Well, what is the problem? Let's get on with this show."

I am now in a state of panic after numerous failed attempts to get my engine started. By now the condom is drying up and looks like it got kicked in the back of the head. Currently, the condom is in the same state as my Johnson; useless and shriveled up. I then try to talk my way out of the situation and call a timeout.

Me: "I am having problem with this condom. I got it from Ray, and I think he got one of those cheap condoms from the clinic or something. But don't worry; I think this can be easily fixed. Hold on, I'll be right back. Don't move. I'm just going to go fix it in the bathroom."

RENE: "OK, just hurry up!"

I head to the bathroom. Right when I get in the bathroom, I wipe my face with towel. I am currently dumfounded as to how I got a serious case of limp dick-itis. This situation has never happened

to me and if I had one wish like Ray J, I would ask for an entrée of Viagra with a side order of Cialis.

Next, I resort to my only option at the time. I look down at Mr. Limp and I give my dick a pep talk as if I am a football coach giving his losing team a halftime speech.

"Come on...you have cum so far and so much this season! It's time to stand up! I have seen you cum from behind...and on top... and on the bottom. Are you just gonna lay down and lets this pussy control you? I know you can do it. I have seen you do it before in the past. This isn't the first time we have played on wet grass. We played last week in Chicago on wet grass and yesterday in LA on wet grass. Put your helmet back on, get back on that field and let's score!"

Needless to say the desperate pep talk didn't work. As a walk out the bathroom, I tell Rene that somehow the condom broke. I explain to her that I need to go get some more condoms in hopes that this will buy me some time and cool me off. More importantly, that Mr. Limp will magically rise like a hot air balloon. I put my clothes back on and let her know that I will be back in ten minutes. As I walk my sweaty self back into the living room I see Ray on the couch watching TV.

RAY: "Look at you! You my friend, have been putting in some serious work. You are sweating all over the place. How was it?"

ME: "How was it? My soldier won't stand at attention! The MOFO is AWOL! It's like I have drunk dick but I'm not drunk. What do I do?"

RAY: "You mean to tell me...that fine ass girl couldn't get you hard? What did you do with the condom I gave you?"

ME: "It's a long story. Any advice on how to get my soldier to salute?"

RAY: "Alright, calm down. Let's take a ride. Is she okay being in there by herself?"

ME: "She should be. She was waiting for me to bring the lightning and the thunder...I couldn't even bring a raindrop nor a gust of wind."

Ray and I squeeze into the infamous Geo Metro and head over to the gas station.

RAY: "Now the first thing you need is some Red Bull. It has wings to make you fly. Cause right now you ain't even walking. Second you need some peppermint gum to give your body the impression that it is cooling down. Third, you need some more condoms because you don't want her pregnant on your first hit."

ME: "OK. I get the condoms and the peppermint gum, but Red Bull? Why Red Bull?"

Ray all of a sudden turns into a Harvard-educated sexologist.

RAY: "Well, what the Red bull does is increase one's heart rate. With the increased heart rate it in turns, increases blood flow. An increased blood flow enables your Peter to Pan. And with a Peter that is Panned, you will have her walking up the walls like she was Spiderman. Not only that, the B6 and B12 vitamins in the drink help to increase stamina. With those types

of vitamins in your system, you will take her to Never
Never Land...trust me."

ME: "You sure this is going to work?"

RAY: "Does a dolphin piss in the ocean? Have I ever
steered you wrong?"

ME: "We shall see."

I bring all my items to the checkout counter. The cashier rings me
up for all three of my recommended items. We jump back into the
car and start driving again.

ME: "I don't believe this happened to me. I have never
been in a situation like this before. The bad thing is that it
is new pussy. Virgin pussy at that."

RAY: "You can't think about that. The only thing that
needs to be on your mind is how you are going to trans-
port this Egyptian girl to Never-Never Land. Hurry up
and down that Red bull. Also, before we head back to the
apartment, you need to take a warm up lap."

ME: "A warm up lap? What is that supposed to mean."

Ray pulls into a Sex Shop parking lot.

ME: "Why are we stopped here?"

RAY: "Because right now, we have to get you focused on
the important things in life. P-U-S-S-and Y. Because you
have a green eyed virgin waiting for you to pile drive her
and you're acting like a bitch. See if you would start hitting
the herb like me, you would never have this problem. I

smoke; I fuck. I fuck and then I smoke. It is like the ying to my yang. I keep life simple. Not this complex, I've fallen and can't get up bullshit that you're on."

We get out of the Geo Metro and walk around the sex shop. I'm looking at magazines and DVD covers feeling like a pervert in a trench coat. After a few minutes of looking at 31 different flavors of pussy, I feel confident to get back to the mission at hand. I have now cooled down from my near death heat exhaustion. We leave the sex shop without purchasing anything, but I have tons of visuals in my head to help me blow this girl's back out.

I arrive back to Ray's bedroom ready for the second half of my sexcapade.

RENE: "What took you so long?"
ME: "I had to stop for gas, but the gas station that I normally go to was closed so I had to find another station."
RENE: "Did you get the condoms? Because I have to go pretty soon."
ME: "Yeah, I got them, and I'm ready for some action."

I look at the clock and see that she has to be home in about 40 minutes so that she doesn't miss her midnight curfew. Like déjà vu, we are at it again. This time, I am on my Dwayne Johnson: hard as a rock. I am ecstatic that all of Ray's tricks are working. I put the condom on my rock. So far so good. I had been waiting for this moment for forever and a day. Then, I get ready to pop the cherry. She asks me to go slow and easy. I'm thinking the opposite, fast and hard. I put my banana in her fruit bowl and we start making fruit

salad. I have now reached my destination: Pussytown, and people in this city are friendly. Maybe a little too friendly. Two minutes into making our fruit salad, I spill all of my ranch dressing. Oh, no, SpaghettiOs!

RENEE: "What's wrong? Why did you stop?"

Embarrassed and fearing that I will get my first BDR (Bad Dick Report), I go with the "morally correct" explanation.

ME: "I...I...I just feel kind of bad."
RENE: "You feel bad? You feel bad about what?"
ME: "See this is your first time having sex. I know that we are not in a relationship or anything and I would hate for you to lose your virginity to me. We should take things a little slower."
RENE: "Well, it is a little too late for that. We were already having sex, and you just can't unscramble eggs! The damage is already done. So let's keep going."
ME: "You're right, but I just think it was not meant to be tonight. Look at the clock...you are supposed to be home real soon. Sex is not something you rush. This is not double dutch where you rush in and rush out. If I didn't care about you I would not be having this conversation. I just think its best that we wait another time when we are not so pressed for time."
RENE: "I guess you're right. This does feel kind of rushed."

Thankfully, she took my bait. We threw our clothes back on, and I walked her to her car. I asked her to send me a text once she got

home. She thought that I was the nicest guy for considering her feelings and making sure she got home at a decent time. Little did she know I went from not being able to get my engine started to becoming the world's next minute man.

Back in the apartment, Ray had post game interview questions for me.

RAY: "So how did my prescription work? Do I know what I'm talking about or do I know what I'm talking about?"
ME: "Your prescription worked a little too well."
RAY: "Did you take her to Never-Never Land?"
ME: "More like Never AGAIN Land. My Peter definitely got Panned but he didn't fly for very long."
RAY: "All that work we did and you had no hang time. HAHAHA. You disappoint me young grasshopper. You have a lot to learn."

Ray ended up watching TV on the couch, and I went to bed. I was so disappointed in my gun for failing me. Needless to say, a week later I was able to have Rene walking up the walls like Spiderman...finally.

The thing about a gun is that it can malfunction when you least expect it too. My gun was no exception. I guess the Never Never Land that Ray spoke of was a mystical place meant to stay in fairytales that day. I know Never Never Land was not a reality for me that night. My Peter was finally Panned and it was an utter disappointment. Rene's snatch was like trying to ride in the Geo Metro. I had problems getting in it, but when I finally made it in, I wasn't in there for long. This story is dedicated to all the guns that have ever malfunctioned and you were unable to take your woman to Never Never Land.

Chapter 5

When The Cops Come Knockin'

Jason and I are getting ready to head out to chase some tail. As we are getting into the car, I get a phone call from Tammy. Jason was one of my closest friends and classmates at the University of Arizona. Jason always knew me to have an attractive woman in the stable and would ask if these women had friends. So while I am on the phone with Tammy, I ask if she has any friends that want to act like a squirrel and play with Jason's nuts. She thinks about it and decides she is going to hook Jason up with her roommate, Stephanie.

Since the point of going out is to crush ass, I figure that I can save time and money by going straight to Tammy's house. The first time I nailed Tammy was easier than trying to remember the number for "911". It was like Domino's Pizza, delivered hot in thirty minutes or less.

One thing about Tammy: she was down for whatever. She was never really in her right mind because she was always high on weed or drunk. I never did that kind of thing but I had fun with the women when they were on it. Tammy was like a porn star in bed. She would fuck, suck, duck, chuck, and let me nut all over her face. I would give her face paintings as if she was at the local county fair.

Tammy was the type that would not mind blowing you while you took a shit. Just a nasty freak. She was a screamer and loved to fuck all day, every day. She fucked when she was bored, she fucked when she was happy, she fucked when she was sad. In her mind she was like Dr. Seuss's Green Eggs n' Ham. She would do it here or there, she would do it anywhere. She would do it in a boat, she would take it in her throat...well, you get the picture.

Now, Jason and I get to Tammy's house. We walk in the house, and the two women are watching the evening news. I introduce Jason to Stephanie and right away there is some sort of mutual attraction. Everyone gets acquainted with each other and Jason goes to the kitchen to start pouring drinks. Vodka and Cranberry juice, a.k.a. the cape cod - the drink that makes all of 'em slob on the knob.

We all had to keep quiet in Tammy's apartment because she had older neighbors and she had really thin walls. An hour later, there is no more cranberry juice and no more liquor. So Jason and Stephanie volunteer to go to the store together and re-up on the pussy potion.

As soon as the door closed, it was on. Tammy jumped on my bone like a stray dog from downtown Tijuana. Her drunken ass started tearing my clothes off and our wrestling match went straight to the bedroom. We are in the bedroom and she is on top of me then I'm on top of her it was as though sex were an Olympic event.

She is screaming at the top of her lungs, and I am feeling like the man. She started getting freakier and cussing me out in Spanish. I don't know what she was saying but whatever it was it

sounded like music to my ears. For all I know she was saying, "Yo quireo Taco Bell." I just know that I was ready to put this sour cream on her taco.

I felt like I just came out of a phone booth with an S on my chest. I wanted to Superman this hoe, *Soulja Boy* style. All of sudden in the middle of my DC Comic performance, I hear banging at the door with my supersonic hearing. I'm disappointed because Jason and Stephanie have just messed up one of my greatest sex sessions.

Tammy and I rock paper scissors for who has to get the door. I naturally go with the symbol that describes my current state. My name at the moment is Chevy, because I am like a Rock. She goes with paper. I lose and then throw my boxers on to answer the door. Then I hear the banging again. This time it is twice louder than before.

> **ME:** "Hold on, Jason! I'm coming...be patient. The pussy is not going anywhere."

I open the door wearing nothing but my boxers, expecting to see Jason and Stephanie. To my surprise it is the boys in blue, Tucson's finest. Both officers have a stern constipated look on their faces.

> **POLICE OFFICER #1:** "Sir, how are you tonight? Are you the owner of this place?"
> **ME:** "No, I am not, I..."

Without asking, Police Officer#2 makes his way in the house, a clear violation of the 4th amendment.

POLICE OFFICER #2: "Sit down on the couch right there. Where is the owner of the apartment?"

The boys in blue look me up and down and see that I am a sweaty mess. Police Officer #1 seems to be more cool and relaxed. Police Officer #2 is buzzed on that drink they call asshole, straight with no chaser. He is on some Hulk mania power trip.

POLICE OFFER#2: "What is your name?"
ME: "Wes Davidson."
POLICE OFFICER#2: "I'm sick of dealing with your kind! Juvenile delinquents. You're never going to learn are you?"
ME: "What are you talking about?"
POLICE OFFICER#2: "Just keep sitting right there on the couch and shut up."

Police Officer#1 tries to cut the tension in the room.

POLICE OFFICER #1: "Sir, is anyone else in the house with you right now?"
ME: "Yes, my friend Tammy is in the back."
POLICE OFFICER #2: "Does she live here?"

I nod my head *yes* as I sit half naked on the couch.

POLICE OFFICER #2: "Tammy, come out here...Now!"

Tammy didn't have time to put her clothes on and was still trying to recover from her pinoche getting annihilated. Tammy walks out

with nothing but a towel on. Both officers gaze at her as if they are sitting front row at the strip club. Officer#1 takes a timid step towards Tammy as if it is his first time asking a stripper for a lap dance avoiding eye contact.

OFFICER#1: "Do you live here ma'am?"
TAMMY: "Yes, I do"
OFFICER 1: "Is everything okay? Do you have any bruises
or scratches on you?"

Officer #2 keeps a close watch on me like a suspect from *America's Most Wanted.*

TAMMY: "Yes, why wouldn't I be?"

Officer#2 cuts off the conversation like an Asian driver and yells from across the room.

OFFICER#2: "Get back in there, and put some damn
clothes on! Then come back out here. We do the questioning around here, not you. As for you Mr. Wes, you just
sit riiiight here and make yourself comfortable. We are
going to get to the bottom of this."

Tammy closes the door and throws some jeans on and comes back out to where all of us are sitting.

Officer#1, still a little intimidated by Tammy's sexiness, explains the situation to her.

OFFICER #1: "We have received an emergency phone call regarding a domestic disturbance. There were screams and the caller claimed it sounded like furniture was moving."

Me being the witty individual that I am, make a smart remark.

ME: "Oh, the furniture was definitely moving"

OFFICER#2: "I told you to shut your trap. Does this seem like a laughing matter to you?"

ME: "No, sir."

OFFICER#1: "Has he hit you or harmed you in any way?"

TAMMY: "No, not at all."

OFFICER#1: "Did you hear any screams?"

TAMMY: "Well...yes that was me, but we were not fighting or anything. We were in my bedroom. Maybe the neighbors heard us."

My mind wondered for a second, and I had just realized that I was going to get arrested for assault. Assaulting the pussy. The officers begin to reconstruct the crime scene in their head. The officers both have an epiphany and realize what is going on: 1) woman naked in the back room with no signs physical abuse 2) I am grinning and still sweaty and 3) there is a condom wrapper in the middle of the living room floor. The conclusion: Suspect is guilty as charged for beating up the pussy. Both officers start laughing hysterically.

Officer#1 walks over to me while I am still sitting on the couch and give me a fist bump.

OFFICER #1: "Wow, you must have been putting in some work. Sounds like you put in more overtime than I did last week on my shift."

Officer#2 acts as if the tampon was taken out of his ass and is still chuckling.

OFFICER#2: "This is the funniest thing that has happened all week. Wait till the guys at the station hear about this one."
OFFICER#1: "We have to get going. You two have a good night...and please try to tame your sex sessions so that we don't have to keep coming out here."

As they are about to exit the apartment and still laughing they stop dead in their tracks. Officer#2 looks as if he has a bad case of the bubble guts. The officer turns on his flashlight and provides a spotlight for a dinner tray containing marijuana seeds next to me on the floor.

Officer#2 leans over near the side of the couch and picks up a roach. The roach he picks up is far from the type that only shows itself when you have company over. This roach was the type that will raise a cop's suspicion and get you locked up. I was completely unaware I had evidence of drug paraphernalia next to me.

Officer#2: "Well, well, well. What do we have here? I see you two are just full of surprises."

I look up at both officers, who are looking at me. I now see myself as a pussy, because I'm about to be fucked. I go over and over in my head as to why I was even messing with Tammy. Then, I remembered: in the bed, her ass was an asset. Outside the bed, I wanted to set her ass.

I came to the realization that I messed with her, because when I was not in her, I was trying to game plan the next time I could be in her. I guess the saying proved to be true. Pussy made the world go around. However, at this point Tammy's pussy was making my world go around a little too much. So much so that it was now becoming a liability.

OFFICER#1: "Who was smoking weed?"

I immediately became the biggest snitch in the room.

ME: "I dunno. But one thing I do know is that it wasn't me."

Tammy immediately shifted the blame from being on us.

TAMMY: "It must have been my roommate, because I have been in my bedroom all night."
OFFICER#1: "Yeah, I kind of figured that through the circumstantial evidence. Mr. Wes over here is sweating like he just got done with a triathlon and your hair is still drenched. Where is your roommate right now?"
TAMMY: "I don't know. I think she went to the store"

Officer#1 must have been feeling generous that day, because he just gave us a warning.

POLICE OFFICER#1: "Well, we are going to let this one go since you guys have been so cooperative, and we have better things to do. Just make sure you get rid of all this

stuff that is not supposed to be here. I was young once, as well. When you decide to do extracurricular activities, you tone it down. That way we don't have to come over here every time you guys are getting busy."

Officer#2 then gives me a quick lecture about how I could have been arrested because drugs were in my vicinity. He scolds the both of us like two red headed stepchildren vying for affection to anyone that will give it them.

> OFFICER#2: "I can book the both of your asses right now! You have to be careful who you associate with. Being dumb will get you locked up. You're lucky my partner is nicer than I am. I don't take any shit."
> ME: "Thank you, officer, for understanding."
> TAMMY: "I really appreciate you not arresting us, officer."
> OFFICER#2: "Don't thank me yet, I need to see both of your IDs. This is just standard procedure since we had to come over here."

I reluctantly hand over my driver's license thinking that I was headed straight for the slammer. Officer#1 calls in over the radio to run a background check. As he runs the background check, Jason and Stephanie walk up to the front door with their hands full of groceries.

> OFFICER#2: "Do you live here?"
> JASON: "No, I don't."

Not realizing what is going on, Stephanie remains quiet.

OFFICER#2: "Well, this is police business that I don't think you want to get involved with right now, so wait outside."

Jason and Stephanie remain calm outside and converse amongst each other. Officer#2 hands me back my license. My license checks out fine. I feel relieved like an 80 year old's bladder at a rest stop on a cross-country road trip. Officer#2's bi-polarism kicks in once again and begins another lecture of the same old stuff.

OFFICER#2: "You should be getting arrested for posses-sion of marijuana. Do you think you're cool because you smoke marijuana?"
ME: "No, sir."
OFFICER#2: "No, as in you don't smoke marijuana or no as in you don't think it is cool?"
ME: "Both sir."

In the middle of Officer#2's 100th lecture of the night, Officer#1 gets of the radio and lets me know that I am free to go. I wish I could say the same thing for Tammy. When Officer#1 ran a back-ground check on Tammy, they discovered that there was a warrant for her arrest.

OFFICER#1: "Ma'am, please turn around. I am placing you under arrest. There is a warrant out for you."
TAMMY: "A warrant? For what?"
OFFICER#1: "Drag racing."

Officer#2 hits her with a verbal jab.

OFFICER#2: "Maybe you shouldn't be driving stick outside the bedroom."

TAMMY: "This must be a mistake. I have never been drag racing!"

OFFICER#1: "Sorry you are going to have to take that up with the courts. But right now we are taking you to jail."

Tammy starts crying in disbelief. With her newly acquired accessories around her wrist, they walk her to the police car. While putting her in the police car, she yells out to me.

TAMMY: "Are you going to pick me up from jail?"

ME: "No, I have a final tomorrow and I need to study."

TAMMY: "You know what. Fuck you, Wes. That is so fucked up."

ME: "Yeah, kind of like your mental state every time I see you. I was not the one drag racing, so drag on deez."

Officer#1 lowers her head in the car and carts her off to the jailhouse. Jason and I leave the crime scene and head home. Once home, I got in bed and begin to stare at the ceiling. I was thankful that I got to spend the night in my own bed with a peace of mind. No drugs, no sex, no alcohol. No more officers and didn't have to worry about an arrest warrant. I laughed to myself and thought about Tammy. Her wild ass began the night riding on my Superman and ended the night riding in a squad car. When the cops come knocking on your door, you better be prepared.

Chapter 6

How I Made Love To A Porn Star

Let's face it, world, people love porn. It is a multi-billion dollar industry. Women like it; men love it. People watch it because they get to fantasize about the person on the screen. So here is the million-dollar question. If you could hook up with your favorite porn star, would you do it? Some would argue that they would never come close to touching them and that they are best to look at...on screen. Some would just do it without hesitation.

As for me, I was always in the middle on the issue. On one side, I was scared that I would catch a STD because of the numerous power tools that are drilled into porn stars every year. On the other side, why not? They are safer than any random groupie running around in the streets. They get tested on a regular basis and cannot perform on screen if their tests come out positive.

In Jenna Jameson's biography, How to Make Love Like a Pornstar, she writes about her struggles growing up and how she eventually became porn star. The title of the book is what drew me in to reading it. It was an interesting read, however, it left me with wondering how do you make Love to a porn star. If I ever got the chance, what was it like to make love to a porn star? And what

type of person would ever get the opportunity? Guess what? I did. Here is my story:

It is 3am and I am watching porn on TV. There is an extremely hot girl on the screen getting slammed like a Blake Griffin fast break. I am watching it not because I am lonely. I am actually at my girl's house and she is asleep in the next room. I came over to her place in the hopes of getting some snatch. Little did I know, she had family in town—good old Aunt Flow. This ruined the whole purpose for me coming over because this law-abiding citizen refuses to run red lights. There is nothing appealing about making love to your girl, turning on the lights only to find yourself in the middle of a crime scene.

I didn't get much slept the night before, and I'm fighting to stay awake. My fight to stay awake consists of my eyes trying their best to close like a convenient store during the the LA riots. I feel like I'm watching a horror movie because this well-known porn star on the flat screen is getting attacked and surrounded by numerous one-eyed dick monsters.

One dick monster is down her throat hitting her tonsils like a speed bag. The other dick monster is attacking her from behind. It is a stick up, and she screams. She grabs another dick monster by the throat and starts to choke the life out of it. In her struggle to choke the one dick monster, he can't take it and throws up on her. As the dick monsters continue to attack her, fatigue sets in on me and like a Metallica song, I fade to black.

I am awoken by laughter coming from the kitchen. As my eyelids struggle to open, I notice that the sun has come out and my girl is getting ready for work.

ME: "What's so funny?"

JORDAN: "Looks like someone forgot to turn off the nude-y show last night."

ME: "Yeah I passed out. Was watching porn, next thing I know porn was watching me."

JORDAN: "Why do you feel the need to watch porn? Am I not enough for you?"

ME: "You are more than enough. But how do you expect me to perform better in bed if I don't watch film? Every great athlete watches film. Film helps to improve technique and shows the proper way to use your stroke."

JORDAN: "Last time I checked...sex was not a sport."

ME: "Sure it is. For one thing, balls are involved, like most sports. It consists of using a stick and placing it in a particular hole. Why do you think after a guy has sex he tells his friends that he's scored?"

JORDAN: "Well, we can talk about this when I get back from work. I am running late, good luck playing pocket pool."

Jordan heads off to work clearly emotional from being on her period. Still groggy, I walk over to my computer and check my MySpace account. As I sign in, I notice that I have a new message from a woman saying hello, who coincidentally looks exactly like the girl on the TV screen last night that got annihilated by the one eyed monsters. However, this woman has a different name and is using the name Krystal.

"This MySpace account has to be spam, or someone is using pictures of my favorite porn star," I tell myself. I wanted to expose this

individual hiding behind the curtain like the Wizard of Oz. I decided to respond back to the alleged imposter with a general message.

ME: "I am doing well; how are you?"

I didn't expect this person to write back, but the way my life has gone, you always expect the unexpected. She writes back.

KRYSTAL: "I am okay. I came across your profile and thought you were a very handsome man."

I am baffled that she wrote back. I am convinced that this is some pervert on the other end trying to mess with my head. Our MySpace exchanges go on throughout the day back, back forth and forth like an Aaliyah song.

As the day comes to a close, my girl gets back home from work and my investigation reveals a few things. This person, by the name of Krystal, lives in LA is a print model, likes to cook, play basketball and go to clubs with her friends. This person just got out of a serious relationship from a well-known producer in the music industry.

Yep, smells like bullshit to me, but at least it kept me entertained throughout the day. That night, as I lay next to my girl, I thought of ways I could prove the person I had been writing to all day was not the person in the pictures. This person was faking the identity of a porn star who signed to Vivid Entertainment, which was the number one porn company in the United States. Why would she be contacting me?

Ah hah, I had an epiphany! I woke up early the next morning to write Krystal a message, but she had already beat me to the punch.

KRYSTAL: "Hope you had a great night last night. You were constantly on my mind from our conversations yesterday. Not only are you fine, you are intelligent. I like a man that is sexy and has brains."

Wow, this imposter is good! He or she knows what to say to try and get a man. One thing is for sure; you can't con a conman. I am no sucker for bullshit. I send my next message just to figure out if this imposter was male or female.

ME: "I am getting tired of writing back and forth. I want to hear your voice."
KRYSTAL: "Sure my number is 213.XXX.XXXX."

Curiosity gets the best of me, and I call as soon as I get her message. It rings, and rings, no answer. *Ah hah!* I knew this person was not who they said they were. I sit back down at the computer and start to write this bitch a nasty message: "I should have exposed you a long time ago. What kind of person sits at a computer pretending to me someone else? You are nothing but a loser, and I hope you..." My phone rings with a 213 number and it is a woman's voice.

ME: "Hello?"
KRYSTAL: "Did someone just call Krystal?"
ME: "Yeah, this is Wes"
KRYSTAL: "Hey, you, sorry I had just bought this new bathing suit and was trying it on. You want to see it?"
ME: "Uh yeah, sure"

KRYSTAL: "OK, I'm going just going to take some pics from my computer since I am right here."

ME: "Alright, call me back."

KRYSTAL: "Oh, you don't want to stay on the phone with me? I can do two things at once you know. Unless, you WANT to get off the phone with me."

True to form, she sends a picture to my inbox of her sitting in her new yellow bikini while holding her cell phone talking to someone. The photos of her match up to the ones on her profile and look exactly like the girl getting nailed in the pornos. The more tests and hoops I put her through, the more her claims are validated. Now the final test as I am still on the phone with her.

ME: "Did you buy anymore bikinis?"

KRYSTAL: "Yeah, I got a blue one and a white one."

ME: "Well, let's chat over the webcam."

KRYSTAL: "OK, hold on, let me sign on."

There is no way she can escape this one.

She signs on to video chat and is wearing the same yellow bikini in her picture. She is holding her cell phone while still talking to me. Everything matched up like a flame at a Texas BBQ. I was now convinced that the porn star and this model were the same girl like an R.Kelly and Usher song.

Now that I had confirmed her identity, I felt more comfortable interacting with her. We spoke constantly when I had breaks during the day while doing various model shoots in LA. Like a lonely woman, she was constantly calling me to see what I was up to.

I was wondering when she was going to tell me what she really did for a living. She was like a super hero who hid her true identity. Only I knew the truth, she was a dick wrangler from the *Wild Wild West*. She would get hit by sperm pistols on a daily basis that would show her no mercy.

Then came my moment of truth: an invitation to her house.

Krystal called me and said that she wanted me to come over and "watch a movie." If you are over 18, then you know what "watch a movie" translates to: *come over so the TV can provide the only light in the room while we play hide the salami.*

She texts me her address and I get going on my way to her place. I had butterflies in my stomach cause I had never been with a porn star. As I am driving over to her place, I call my good friend, Parker.

> ME: "Remember the porn star I was telling you about? I am on my way to her house. Should I blow her brains out or should I just hangout tonight?"
>
> PARKER: "Dude, there is not going to be any brains being blown out. She is a pro. It's going to be like bringing a knife to a gunfight. Your gonna get worked dude."
>
> ME: "Thanks for having confidence in me, life coach."
>
> PARKER: "How can you compete when she is involved in a career where she has to get pile driven by 13-inch cocks? Having sex with her is going to be like throwing a hotdog down a hallway. Not only that; you will contract more diseases than a third world science experiment gone bad. You should pass on the pussy if you know what is good for you."

ME: "I mean, I am going to wear a condom."
PARKER: "That condom better be built Ford tough, I'm talking titanium steel. I wouldn't touch her with a ten-foot pole attached to a ten foot pole. She may be hot but her pussy might be hot as well. It's not worth it dude."

After hanging up the phone with Parker, I decide to go to her dwelling place anyway.

When Krystal opened her front door to let me in, she was wearing some boy shorts and a tank top with no bra. Her outfit was screaming, "Welcome, Mr. Wes, I am the valet attendant for hard cocks. Your number is 121,313,131. Thank you for visiting the Jizz Carlton, enjoy your stay." All that was needed was a sound bite from Miles Lane saying, "Let's get it on."

As I walked through the door, she invited me right to her bedroom. Next, threw me the remote to the huge flat screen in front of her bed.

KRYSTAL: "Watch whatever you want. I just got out the shower."
ME: "And...I didn't get an invite because..."
KRYSTAL: "Because I don't know you like that."

The thing that pisses me off is when hoes try to act like something they are not. Now all of a sudden Krystal is in the running for the moral character of the year award. An average day at work for her is getting rammed like St. Louis.

ME: "True, you don't know me like that but at least you could have seen what I was working with."

KRYSTAL: "Trust me, I have seen everything."
ME: "I definitely believe you on that."
KRYSTAL: "What is that supposed to mean?"
ME: "Meaning you are a pretty girl; I'm sure that you have had
an opportunity at tons of guys throwing themselves at you."

What I really meant to say was: "WTF do you think it means? You
interact with more cocks than Ol McDonald on his farm, E-I-E-HOE."

KRYSTAL: "Aww, thank you, you are so sweet. How was
your day, today? You actually look a little tense. Why don't
you lie down so I can give you a massage?"
ME: "Do I get a happy ending?"
KRYSTAL: "Maybe, depends how well behaved you are."

Krystal walks over, opens the top drawer of the nightstand next
to her bed, grabs the remote from me, turns the TV off, and lights
a candle.

KRYSTAL: "What kind of music do you like? I have some
stuff that hasn't been released yet that my ex sent to me."
ME: "Sounds good me."

Krystal turns the music on and removes my shirt. She proceeds
to give me one of the best massages that I have ever had in my life
which she follows up with sucking on my ears and my neck. She
flips me over and starts to massage my chest.

KRYSTAL: "Let me make you a little more comfortable."

Next, Krystal removes my belt and slides off my jeans, then my boxers, and I am laying there with my pecker screaming, "Suck me! Suck me!" She interrupts her sexual seduction and jumps off of me. Then, she starts giving me a strip tease at the edge of the bed while the music plays in the background.

> **KRYSTAL:** "Ohh I love this song!"
> **ME:** "I like this song too, but you just stopped everything right when it was starting to get good. You can't stop a fireworks display during the Fourth of July! "
> **KRYSTAL:** "We have a long night, just be patient."

She completely goes off the topic like she has ADD.

> **KRYSTAL:** "I have been really trying to gain weight by doing a lot of squats at the gym. I have been working on my ass, what do you think?"

Krystal takes her boy shorts off, revealing that she was not wearing any panties. She bends over in front of me and I feel like a TSA agent, because I can see all of her paraphernalia.

> **ME:** "What do I think? I think I am ready to tap that, if fucking you is wrong then I don't want to be right...Please don't say I'm right."

Krystal laughs hysterically. She then takes her top off and starts to dance like a tenured stripper. She sits on my knee and starts

grinding on it. She then spreads her pussy lips apart and reveals her hole like it is a grade school show and tell day.

KRYSTAL: "Do you like what you see?"
ME: "Stevie Wonder would like what he sees right about now!"
KRYSTAL: "I want to show you something else."
ME: "I don't think there is anything else to show. I think when you bent over in front of me I saw all the way up to your throat."
KRYSTAL: "You are so crazy! Watch this."

Krystal walks over to her nightstand and opens her bottom drawer. This drawer is filled up to the brim with sex toys. I had never seen so many different sex toys in one drawer. It looked like something out of the Ringling Brothers Circus.

After seeing this magnificent treasure chest, I start singing the Toys R Us song in my head. "I don't want to grow up I'm a Toys 'R Us kid there's a million toys in that drawer that I can play with. From vibrators to freaky clothes to dildos at the biggest toy store there is. I don't wanna grow up, cause if I did, I couldn't be a Toys 'R Us kid."

What occurred next could have been called by Chris Berman over at ESPN: *This just in... Krystal "the lover of the penis pistol" calls the audible. She takes a transparent vibrator out and puts it in her ass. She takes out a black dildo from the treasure chest. We'll call it da Oakland Raiderrrr. She drops back and does some magic tricks that would make the great Houdini jealous.*

*She places the dildo inside of her. She pushes it back, back back... It....could...go...all...the...way.....**it does**! It disaaaapears! Now you see it, now you don't. Krystal then contracts her pussy muscles back and forth and makes her pussy talk as if it is one of Jim Henson's Muppets— Lookma no hands! Rumblin', stumblin, bumblin' and a little coochie rubbing. Next, she pulls the dildo out like a rabbit out of a hat. She puts the transparent vibrator in her mouth. Whooooop! Whooooop!*

You can see Wes' winky dinky; look at it grow! She turns over to show her caboose. Wes slaps the caboose. Nobody circles that wagon like Wes does. That's why she plays this game.

She is ready for me to enter in her garden of love, and I am ready to manicure her lawn. Then, I have a vivid flashback come across me in the form of Parker's voice. "She may be hot, but her pussy may be hot as well. It's not worth it, dude." I freeze. I sit there motionless and stop myself from taking it any further.

ME: "I can't do this right now."

KRYSTAL: "What's wrong? Did I scare you off?"

ME: "No. It's just I also got out of a serious relationship, and I still have feelings for my ex."

KRYSTAL: "That is understandable, just lay back and relax. I will make you forget all about her."

Krystal pushes me back on the bed. She starts to play my flute elegantly as if she is member of the Symphony Orchestra. She does it so well that I can feel tingling in my toes. I stop her once again.

ME: "I really have to get going."

I walk over to the other side of the bed and put my clothes back on. She is sitting there in shock. Her mouth is wide open like it is in many of her pornos that I am all too familiar with. I end up leaving her place without finishing the game I had set out to play. I gave up in the middle of foreplay. I had disappointed myself and canceled my own Fourth of July fireworks. Like a Sugar Ray Leonard vs. Roberto Duran fight, I essentially told her, "No Mas." I let doubt get the best of me and I froze up during my million dollar shot. Thanks, Parker.

I called her a week later to try again. She surprisingly answered.

> **KRYSTAL:** "Hey, stranger, haven't heard from you in awhile."
> **ME:** "What are you doing later? I'm ready for a rematch."

Like a championship boxer denying a challenger another shot at the title, she respectfully declines.

> **KRYSTAL:** "Actually, I decided to get back with my ex, so I can no longer see you."

Did I just get stiff armed by a porn star who, all of a sudden, had morals? That question can be answered in the affirmative. Maybe I hurt her pride; maybe she had too many other lollipops to suck on. Who knows? I do know my investigation left me empty-handed, and I never learned how to make love to a porn star nor how to make love like a porn star.

Like a sports fan, all I can do now is watch the action from the TV screen. However, I know it is a different game when you are on the field actually playing in the game. I had my chance; it

came and went. I am still left wondering; how do I make love like a porn star? So Jenna Jameson, if you are reading this, please teach me how to make love like a Porn star. I tried to teach myself and failed miserably. I guess sometimes you win, sometimes you lose and sometimes you just freeze up in the face of pussy.

CHAPTER 7

She Likes It Doggy Style

I was in Florida for a week to watch the Super Bowl. If you have never been to a city when it hosts a Super Bowl, I highly recommend it. Usually, the city that hosts the Super Bowl is full of one-night stands and drunken groupies for everyone. It brings a new meaning to the term "the freaks come out at night".

I met Stacy at Victoria's Secret in the mall during the middle of day. I saw her walk into Victoria's Secret, so I followed her in. While browsing for a set of pajama bottoms, I approached her.

ME: "Hi."

She gave me the "who is this retard?" look and reluctantly replied.

STACY: "Umm. Hi."

I extended my hand with a friendly smile to let her know that I was hitting on her.

ME: "My name is Wes; what's your name?"
STACY: "Stacy, and my last name is, *I have to get going*."
ME: "Ouch! You are a feisty one, Miss I-have-to-get-going."

STACY: "I just don't have time for guys right now, but you seem really nice."

I noticed that her key chain had a picture of a Chihuahua on it. I had just found my "in" and quickly concocted a story.

ME: "I was just going to ask you if you knew of any dog parks nearby where I could take Denver."
STACY: "Denver?"
ME: "My apologizes. Denver is the name of my puppy"
STACY: "Oh really? How old is he?"
ME: "He is a four-month-old Lab."
STACY: "I love it when they are that age. I have a three-year-old Chihuahua named Tabitha. She is my heart. Do you want to see a picture of her?"
ME: "Sure."

Stacy eagerly held up her key chain so I could see her pooch.

ME: "Wow, she is really pretty."

Sometimes I can't believe the lies guys tell in order to get a woman. I acted like I was interested in her little pooch, but in actuality, I hate Chihuahuas. They remind me of a rat on HGH. Chihuahuas are like A-cup tits; they always wish they were a lot bigger than what they really are.

It is funny how a conversation can turn so quickly because, within seconds, Stacy was all of a sudden interested in what I had to say.

STACEY: "This is Victoria's secret. May I ask what you are doing in here? Let me guess, shopping for a girlfriend?"
ME: "To be honest, I followed you in here. But only because I wanted to know if you could put on an outfit for me. I promise I'm not some creep, I just have a friend that has the same body type as you and I want to get her something that fits perfectly."
STACY: "Ha, nice try buddy! And what makes you so special? Get out of here, that is the oldest trick in the book. I'm not falling for that one...good try though."

Trying to redeem myself, I think of a quick comeback.

ME: "It's not what you think. You see, Victoria Secret has a new clothing line called the Birthday Suit edition. I am from out of town and they only carry that line in this area. The Birthday Suit Edition is only offered for a limited time. Actually, only offered as long as you are standing in front of me. I think you should take off what you have on and put on the Victoria's Birthday Suit."
STACY: "Really?"

I can no longer hold in my laughter and Stacy gets my joke.

STACY: "You are crazy. I can't believe I fell for that one."

A little more small talk and I walk out of Victoria's Secret with Stacy's number. I called her that evening to see if she knew of any parties going on in the city. My phone call reveals that she is a Jacksonville

Jaguar cheerleader and works part time as a dental assistant. I noticed that Stacy had low self-esteem for as pretty as she was. She was insecure about her looks and needed everyone to tell her how pretty she was. She was naive and not the smartest cookie in the cookie jar. She was a few fries short of a happy meal and the epitome of a bimbo. There seemed to be something off about Stacy but I could not place my finger on the exact issue. After talking over the phone a few times, Stacy invited me over one night. I input her address in my GPS and drove my rental car to her house.

I arrived at Stacy's condo and rang the doorbell. From where I was standing, I could hear the ferocious guard dog, Tabitha. Stacy cracked opened the door in order to prevent Tabitha from getting out. The best weatherman couldn't have prepared me for what happened next. Tabitha sprinted toward my shoes and started sniffing them. Then she let out a monstrous sneeze, which consisted of Chihuahua mucus and a side order of doggy slobber. My right shoe went from black patent leather to snotty glazed in a matter of seconds.

STACY: "I'm so sorry, Tabitha has a bit of a cold. Here let me get a towel to wipe that off. Come on in. Please take your shoes off because we just installed new carpet."

Stacy and I head to the kitchen where she wiped the phlegm off of my shoe.

ME: "I didn't know dogs got sick like that."
STACY: "Yeah, they are just like people."

Stacy bent over towards Tabitha and went into baby talk mood.

STACY: "My baby is just so sick, huh? Well, we are just
going to have to get better aren't we? Oh, yes, we are."

Tabitha responded with a bark as if she understood every word Stacy
had just said. In reality, Tabitha understood Stacy just as well as an
American could understand Chinese on in his first day of Mandarin
class. Stacy invited me upstairs to her room to watch some TV
because she didn't want to disturb her roommate who was in the
living room catching the last 15 minutes of Friends. While walking
up the stairs, Tabitha followed suit. I could see that trying to get rid
of Tabitha was going to be like trying to get a blemish off of your
credit report. It just wasn't going to happen.

We get to her room and stretch out on her bed. Tabitha
jumps on the bed and lays at the edge of Stacy's feet. We watch TV
for a bit then we start making out. Tabitha sees what we are doing and tries to jump in the action. Sorry, bitch, three's a crowd in
this situation. I gently shove Tabitha back. Tabitha doesn't take no
for an answer and comes back like a boomerang. She starts licking
Stacy's face and comes over to me. This time, I give her a stern
shove in order to get her away from me. It may have been a little
too stern. A loud thud could be heard as Tabitha went airborne
and hit the floor. Stacy, stops sucking face with me.

STACY: "What was that?"
ME: "Bass. I heard it as well. Probably someone's car
stereo while driving by."

Stacy looks around and sees Tabitha on the side of the bed jumping up and down trying her best to get back on the love boat. Stacy goes back to her annoying baby voice and talks to Tabitha.

STACY: "Precious, did you fall off of the bed and hurt your little head?"

Stacy points across the room to the doggy bed.

STACY: "Go over there and lay down until mommy can take care of you."

Tabitha walks over and lies down on her bed. Stacy and I get back to sucking face. After subtracting a substantial amount of clothing, we are in our birthday suits. Now that we are in our birthday suits we engage in some foreplay then move on to a certain type of sex style paying tribute to Tabitha—the doggy style.

I am in her land of OZ; call me Toto. As I continue burying my bone in her yard, I feel a tingling in my feet. The tingling at my feet happens to be Tabitha. She is licking my feet as if they were Scooby snacks. I then furnish a back kick that would have made Mr. Ed jealous. Unfortunately, Tabitha was on the other end of that back kick and produced another thud sound effect when she hit the floor.

To my dismay, Tabitha bounced back from the canvas. She was back in business and back on the bed. She must have hit her head pretty hard on the floor because she got up thinking she was a chef. Chef Tabitha then attempted to toss my salad. I tried to fan her away from behind as if she was a stinky fart. However, this clever critter got through my defense and went straight for my

chicken nuggets. The move by Tabitha startled me so bad I completely stopped my stroke and took my bone out of Stacy's biscuit.

ME: "What the—"
STACY: "Just relax, she means no harm. See..."

Tabitha runs up to Stacy and licks her inner thigh. Just as Tabitha moves closer to licking Stacy's biscuit, Stacy picks Tabitha up.

STACY: "Just let her stay on the bed. You might like it."
ME: "Your dog just tried to lick my ball sack. I can't concentrate when Fido is trying to have a three-some with me."
STACY: "Come on, what guy doesn't like having his balls licked during sex?"
ME: "That might be true but not by the taco bell dog."
STACY: "She is not just a dog. She is my baby...Fine I will put her on the floor."

Stacy instructs Tabitha to get back in the doggy bed and tells her to stay. Tabitha reluctantly listens.

Finally, I am back on the gravy train and back in her *Newfoundland*. This time I decide to attack her puppy pound like a *Pit Bull*. I have a feeling that I am about to *Whippet* good. I come fast out of the gates, like a *Greyhound* racing champ. This causes her to make sounds like a drunken *Bloodhound*. I can tell she is enjoying my *Cocker Spaniel* because she is telling me to keep giving it to her big like a *Great Dane*.

She must have thought I had a *Miniature Schnauzer*. While giving it to her hard, she tries to scoot forward and away from me so

I had to *Boxer* in. I then grabbed both of her breasts from behind. While my fingertips were on her nipples I did like a *Doberman* and *Pinscher*. I looked down at her ass and it was rippling like a *Shar Pei*. Fifteen minutes into me destroying her *Chow Chow*, Stacy and I are panting like *Alaskan Snow Dogs*. She opens her mouth as she cums and tries to talk, but clearly, she is *Alaskan Mala-mute*.

Soon after she cums, I join her. I spill my kibbles and bits in her doggie bowl. It's good thing that I had my dogcatcher over my *Rottweiler* because my milk bone shot out enough kibbles and bits for a litter of puppies. I get up and throw my dogcatcher in the waste basket.

Stacy's roommate had now left so we head downstairs to put on a movie in the DVD player since Stacy didn't have a player in her room. While we are enjoying the rest of our night watching a movie, I hear a growling from the top the stairs.

ME: "What is Tabitha growling at? Is this place haunted?"
STACY: "No, she is just pissed that I made her get on the floor, when you were giving it to me daddy."
ME: "I have never seen a dog so jealous."

As I look up from the couch, I notice Tabitha with my used raincoat in her mouth. She is shaking it violently while simultaneously splashing my DNA all over the walls and new carpet. At least the new interior designer knew how to coordinate the proper colors.

ME: "Stacy...I think you may want to get your dog. She is having a semen balloon fight with the wall."
STACY: "A semen balloon fight?"

I point towards the top of the stairs. Stacy screams from where we are sitting.

STACY: "Tabitha, no. Drop it, now!"

Tabitha immediately drops the condom from her mouth. Tabitha then goes to plan B and starts licking up the remains of my human milkshake from the carpet.

STACEY: "Tabitha, get down here!"

An excited Tabitha picks up her new play toy and sprints down the stairs. Tabitha jumps in between where Stacy and I are sitting. Stacy tries to take the condom out of Tabitha's mouth. However, Tabitha thinks they are in the final championship game of tug-the-jimmy. Stacy tries her best to pull the condom out of Tabitha's mouth. Tabitha doesn't budge; she growls and pulls back even harder. Tabitha gains a little traction and puts her two hind legs in reverse.

STACY: "Let go, Tabitha!"

Tabitha refuses to let go and stretches the condom even further. The stretched out condom is now covered in slobber sauce with a hint of Wes semen. Stacy loses her grip and the condom slips out of her hand. The condom goes flying and Tabitha gets a taste of a smack-a-bitch sandwich right across her whiskers. Tabitha lets out a big yelp and finally drops the rubber. Stacy rushes over and picks up the wounded pooch.

STACY: "I'm so sorry princess."

Stacy starts to kiss Tabitha on the cheek. Tabitha uses her cum drenched tongue and starts licking Stacy all over her mouth. Stacy sets Tabitha back down and instructs the dog to go upstairs and lie in her bed. As Tabitha runs up to the bed, Stacy tries to cuddle with me on the couch.

STACY: "I know my puppy acts a little strange when guys are around. Thank you for understanding."

ME: "Puppy? That dog is three years old! I think she is full grown. I don't understand why she acts like that. That is one horny dog. I have seen dogs act horny, but she is on another level. It's as if you feed her estrogen tablets every day."

STACY: "I can explain. Can you keep a secret?"

ME: "Sure."

STACY: "OK...you ready for this?"

ME: "Yeah, what is it?"

STACY: "Well...I use to get really horny after I broke up with my last boyfriend. I hated men and never wanted to be with one again."

ME: "That's no big deal; I think that is normal when people get hurt in relationships-"

STACY: "I'm not finished."

ME: "Sorry, go ahead."

STACY: "Well, I would wake up in the middle of the night and my body would get all tingly inside. I wanted dick, but at the same time, I was scared to be with someone."

My assumption of something being amiss from the beginning of our relationship seems to be coming true. This cheerleader is not right in the head.

ME: "I don't like how this story is going…"

STACY: "Just hear me out. I would go downstairs to the kitchen and…"

ME: "Oh, so you are an emotional eater. Let me guess, you have an eating disorder like the rest of the cheerleading squad?"

STACY: "You are still not listening!"

ME: "OK, I promise to listen this time; I just got caught up in the moment."

STACY: "Speaking of getting caught up in the moment, that is what would happen to me. I would go down to the kitchen open the cabinet and get the peanut butter. I would bring it to bed with me. I would sit there and watch TV and eat the peanut butter right out of the jar. Tabitha would sit there and beg for the peanut butter."

ME: "I was wondering why Tabitha would get so crazy when we were in the bed together. She wanted her peanut butter."

STACY: "Yeah but there is one thing that I left out. I would watch porn on my TV, and then I would put the peanut butter all over my clit so that Tabitha would lick it clean."

ME: "As in, you trained her to lick your pussy whenever you were in bed?"

I could not believe what I was hearing. Tabitha was trained to eat pussy. I had heard of dogs eating pussies, but those were actual felines. This was the first time I had heard of a dog eating human pussy.

ME: "Remind me to never let you make me a PB&J sandwich. That can't be normal. Did your last ex-boyfriend know about this?"

STACY: "Yes, he would like it."

ME: "He would?"

STACY: "Of course, what guy doesn't want his balls licked while having sex."

ME: "You mentioned that Tabitha liked balls but I had no idea you meant these kinds of balls."

STACY: "Wes, you are so uptight when it comes to sex, why don't you just live a little?"

ME: "What else did your ex like?"

STACY: "One time he asked me to take a shit on him."

ME: "A shit? Like a South Park, Mr. Hankey type shit?"

STACY: "Yeah, exactly"

ME: "And you did it?"

STACY: "Yeah, he was laying down in the bathtub and he begged for me to do it, so I did it."

At this point, I was sick to my stomach like an international tourist who had just eaten street meat in Juarez, Mexico. I was speechless. I had heard of stories of guys liking that kind of thing but never thought that any of those stories were true. I guess I had been proven wrong. It was now time for me to make my exit strategy.

ME: "You know what? It is getting kind of late and I have a long day tomorrow...You know the Super Bowl being tomorrow and everything."

STACY: "OK, I will walk you out. Just give me a call tomorrow when you get settled."

I left that night and wondered if Stacy went back to her room so that she could make PB&P (Peanut Butter & Pussy) sandwiches for Tabitha. I caught a flight out of Jacksonville a few days later. Thank you Stacy for scarring me for life. Every time I turn on a Jacksonville Jaguar game, and the network cuts to a sideline shot of the cheerleaders, one thought comes to mind PB&P sandwiches and the cheerleader who liked them doggy style.

Chapter 8

Not So Perfect Planning

Brittany and I had been seeing each other for a few months now. Brittany is a woman who thinks she is better than everyone else because she has certain moral standards. Brittany is the type of girl that loves sex but at the same time is worried about getting her "numbers up". Meaning, when she gets married she wants to be able to count on one hand the amount of men that have pounded her porridge. We met in the bookstore, of all places, and at the time she had a boyfriend.

She gave me her number, I asked her out, and she told me that she could not go on a "date" with me but would be willing to go to lunch anytime I wanted. It was the same thing; only she could not put the word "date" on whatever it was we were doing because she didn't want to disrespect her boyfriend. Morals are kind of like religion, people use them when it's convenient in order to feel good about themselves.

I wined and dined her and told her how much fun I had hanging out with her. I was basically being a sucker for love. You know all the pathetic things men try to do to get that one piece of ass. As for myself, I am competitive so I continue to try until I have I have another notch under my belt. In the past, I have been patient enough to wait for months for a woman to let me enter into her

fountain of love. Patience is like a hungry dog without a leash, he will usually always get the pussy in front of him.

I had been trying to bang Brittany going on seven months now. What was preventing her from letting this iron sheik penetrate her camel toe? I was not her "boyfriend". We would often get to the point where she got butt naked in my bed then she would treat me like Cam Newton and award me her best impression of the Heisman Trophy. I would often hear three words—no, don't, and stop—and about 100 stiff arms later, Brittany asks me if I could drop her off at the airport. She tells me her flight is leaving at 4:00pm and I make plans to be there at noon because this girl was a stickler for time.

Brittany is the type of girl I call the perfect planner. These girls have type-A personalities and everything must go according to how they planned it. They are the polar opposite of a spontaneous person. Brittany had to plan everything from the moment she woke up in the morning to the time she had to take a shit. Brittany was on some *One Who Flew Over the Cuckoo's Nest* type shit. Brittany would try to plan a planner. This woman would plan things that were not meant to be planned for. If something was not planned in Brittany's life, she would panic and even try to plan when she was stressed.

I arrived to Brittany's place at noon. To my surprise she still had a few more things to pack. I'm sitting on her bed waiting for her to get the last of her things together. Then all of a sudden she makes a seven-word statement that is music to a man's ears: "I want to have sex with you." I give her the kind of look an ugly girl gives a guy who has just told her how pretty she is. Not really believing it but hoping that it is true.

ME: "You want to have sex with me right now?"

BRITTANY : "Yes...right now!"

ME: "Where is this coming from all of the sudden?"

BRITTANY: "You know I plan everything and I had to plan the first time we have sex. Hurry up and take your clothes off before I have a change of plans. My hormones are raging! I know you are not my boyfriend but this will be the first time I'm having sex with someone who is not my boyfriend."

Did this girl just "plan" a cheating session with me on her boyfriend? What I have learned in life is that every female will manipulate to get what she want. Brittany at this movement, is lying about the first time cheating on her boyfriend so she can get her world rocked like me.

In this situation I have three options:

A) Call her out and tell her she is full of shit.

B) Try to be the nice guy and do the morally right thing by telling her that we shouldn't sleep together be-cause she has a boyfriend at home who is in madly in love with her.

C) Just do like I have been doing and go along with the warped way this cuckoo thinks. I can act like I really care about her and that way I can fuck her like she stole my fifth grade lunch money.

Yep, you guessed it, I went with choice C.

We end up passionately kissing and she is ripping my clothes off as I rip off hers. It was somewhat of a steamy love scene like in

the skin flick movies. Somewhere between late night Cinemax and hardcore porn. Our love scene goes back and forth like a tennis match at Wimbledon. She kisses my top lip, I kiss her bottom lip. She feels up my chest like cardiologist, I rub her breasts like a perverted masseuse. She unzips my pants. I unbutton her pants. I reach for her York Peppermint Pattie, she pulls out my Mr. Goodbar. She can no longer take the back and forth banter in this tennis match and begs for me to satisfy her needs. Brittany anxiously hands me a condom. I gladly put my raincoat on like I'm walking around Seattle, Washington cause this is about to be a wet storm.

I have now reached my destination and it is everything I had thought it would be and more. I was finally in the cookie jar. After a few strokes and after getting done with my warm up lap, I hear man's most dreaded word in the English language:

BRITTANY: "Stop!"
ME: "Stop? What do you mean stop?"

I do like a forensic detective and try to analyze the scene. I begin to put the pieces together and try to determine where I went wrong. Was I too aggressive? Was this not what she wanted? Is this perfect planner about to charge me with rape, so I can have a perfect jail sentence?

BRITTANY: "Yes, I said stop"
ME: "What did I do?"
BRITTANY: "Nothing, I need a break."
ME: "A break? Two minutes have not even gone by, and you already need a break?"

Brittany needs a break? What is going on with this cuckoo? One minute she is saying she wants it now she is saying she doesn't! Then she makes a confession.

BRITTANY: "I am really feeling faint. Uh, I think I'm going to faint."

Brittany puts the backside of her palm over her head as if she has a fever. In my head I am thinking I am the man because I just wore this poor little thing out in a matter of minutes. However, she continues her confession.

BRITTANY: "I'm Hypoglycemic."
ME: "Hypo-what?"
BRITTANY: "Hypoglycemic."
ME: "What is Hypogly-"
BRITTANY: "Hypoglycemic. It means that if my blood sugar gets too low then I will pass out."
ME: "How did you get it?"
BRITTANY: "I dunno, I just know I didn't eat today and I'm feeling faint."

This can't be happening to me right now. Here I am in some seven-month-old marinated pussy. I am only on my warm up lap and my tennis event is now canceled due to unforeseen conditions. What part of the planning phase is this?

While my Mr. Goodbar was still in his raincoat, I had to think fast. Next, I sprint like Usain Bolt being chased by a 200-pound Rottweiler to the kitchen looking for anything to bring her blood sugar up. I

frantically open and close cabinets in her kitchen. Naked as a jaybird, I search through every nook and cranny like an officer with a search warrant. I yell from the kitchen on behalf of my dick in distress.

ME: "You have any juice in the fridge?"

With the faintest voice Brittany responds.

BRITTANY: "There are Capri Suns in the cabinet to the left of the fridge."

I open the cabinet and tear open the box of Capri Suns like a fat kid opening a Twinkie at lunchtime. I rush back to the bed and I instruct her to drink the juice as fast as she can. Soon after she downs it, I scramble back to the kitchen and grab another Capri sun. Capri Suns are like giving CPR to your blood sugar.

The current scene feels like a Nascar pit stop: a whole lot of running around within a confined space and feeling the pressure of precious seconds ticking away. After a few seconds pass, she seems to come to life. I am now ready to get my car back on her speedway.

I jump back in the driver's seat and weavr in her traffic. Up and down, in and out, pedal to the medal. My hips accelerate at lightning speed, fearful that my Indy 500 race will be cut short again by the word "stop." While in the 6th gear, I can finally feel the checkered flag waiving neat the finish line. As...I...reach...the... finish...line...

BRITTANY: "Stop!"

I completely mash my brakes.

> **ME:** "Again?"
> **BRITTANY:** "I think I'm going to pass out again. I'm so sorry."
> **ME:** "But I was just about to finish! You have more stop
> and goes than an Asian on his first day of driver's training."
> **BRITTANY:** "I really need to eat something. The Capri Suns
> aren't working that well."

At this point I am frustrated so I run back to the kitchen. At last...
Rice Krispy Treats. Full of sugar, lots of carbs for energy and they
taste good. I rush back to the bed and open the treats.

> **ME:** "Hurry eat this!"
> **BRITTANY:** "I feel so bad that all this is happening."
> **ME:** "Don't talk, you might be wasting energy. You wasting
> energy is not part of the *plan*. I *planned* on finishing what
> we started but that seems to be an issue."
> **BRITTANY:** "You don't have to be a jerk about it!"
> **ME:** "Just eat. I see hypoglycemia makes people moody."

Brittany still has a mouthful of Rice Krispy Treats in her mouth.

> **BRITTANY:** "Just come back over here and put it back in."

Once again, I jump back in the bed for my third try as Brittany is
downing Rice Krispy Treats and washing them down with Capri
Sun juice. I am now back in action, back in her speedway. At this
moment I have made more comebacks than a Brett Farve career.

She is multi-tasking while on her back. Both of her legs are in the air like TV antennas. My car is in her garage hitting on all cylinders. One of her hands is on my back holding on for the ride of her life. The other hand is wrapped around the hypoglycemic antidotes. Half of a Capri Sun and a quarter Rice Krispy square. I guess it is true what they say, America's Got Talent. Now, there is no stopping me thanks to this emergency food. Meanwhile, Brittany's eyes are rolling in the back of her head and I can't tell if she is passing out or it is feeling good to her.

I am coming around the corner for the final stretch. The finish line is in my view and I'm ready to explode like C-4. I have waited ages for the day I would be able to put my fuel injector in her engine. I can now feel my transmission fluid about to leak all over her engine. Then I get blindsided again.

BRITTANY: "We have to stop."
ME: "Stop? Again? I thought you were feeling better. You need me to grab some more Rice Krispy Treats?"
BRITTANY: "No thank you. It's not that."
ME: "Is it me?"

Brittany points across the room to the clock on the wall.

BRITTANY: "I'm going to miss my flight. We have to leave right now."
ME: "Can't you just take the next flight out and say you missed this one?"
BRITTANY: "Oh no, that is not happening. **I DIDN'T PLAN FOR THAT!**"

I, regretfully, got dressed and rushed to take Brittany to the airport. Although I never made it to the finish line that day, I still made it on the speedway. A few weeks later after she made it back in town, I was able to finish what we had started. But only because she was able to plan it!

Chapter 9

Now I Know My ABC's

The ABC song is one of the first songs we learn in grade school. This song brings back not only grade school memories but memories of hanging out Ethan's house. Therefore, to honor Ethan, this funny sex story will be told using the ABCs.

A- As the world turned, so would the stripper around the pole in Ethan's living room.   Ethan's house was a place where a lot of illegal debauchery occurred. Ethan was a wealthy colleague of mine and loved to do wild and crazy things that only his money would allow.   Ethan was armed with the three of the most dangerous self-inflicting weapons a man could have. Power, money, and women.

B- Brad on the other hand was a lot more conservative. Brad was one of Ethan's close friends. Although he was not as wild as Ethan, he was still very competitive when it came to gambling. Often times, they would get into these outrageous bets. Most of these bets were so creative that they could only come from the mind of Ethan.

C- Creative bets are like strippers. They can make life exciting for the moment but if you are not careful, you can blow all your money by the end of the night. One memorable bet occurred during the week between himself and Brad.

D- During a Tuesday playoff game between the Miami Heat and Boston Celtics, Ethan, Brad and I are sitting on the couch eating popcorn.

ETHAN: "I got 300 on Miami. Any takers? Loser has to pay his debt by the end of the week."

E- Ethan is originally from Miami and always roots for his home team. Being the competitive one out of the group Brad shakes Ethan's hand and concurs to the bet. Consequently, the Celtics end up winning and Ethan loses the bet. Soon after the game, a bitter Ethan tells us that he needs to get some sleep and we all go our separate ways.

F- Friday arrives and we are all back at Ethan's house on the couch. Brad brings up the bet from Tuesday.

BRAD: "I know somebody needs to pay up! The way those Celtics put a whooping on the Heat, someone should be paying me double."

G- Giggling like an evil villain, Ethan gets up from the couch and walks into the next room. Meanwhile, Brad taunts Ethan.

BRAD: "What are you laughing at? You owe me money! Laugh at the three hundred dollars that are about to leave your wallet. I could use an extra three hundred dollars. I was thinking of buying that new iPhone. Even better, I will just call the strippers over from last week. Have 'em give me a special lap dance and then make it rain on 'em. Thanks Ethan! I hate to steal money from you but you set yourself up for that one. Who in their right mind goes for Miami?"

Ethan shouts from the other room.

H- He surprisingly concedes to paying his money.

ETHAN: "Don't worry; I am going to pay every penny of it."

I- I don't know what was funnier. The smirk on Ethan's face or Brad's jaw hitting the floor once Ethan came back into the room. True to his word, Ethan paid every penny of his obligation. He literally paid every penny. Apparently earlier that week, Ethan went to bank and requested 300 dollar in pennies. Ethan entered the room holding three large white paint buckets. Each of the three buckets contained 10,000 pennies.

J- Jokingly, Ethan makes a *smart alec* remark to Brad.

ETHAN: "I don't know about making it rain for the strippers but you can definitely make it hail, Mr. Weatherman! Here is your money paid in full."

Brad: "I'm not taking that."
Me: "You guys did agree on three hundred dollars. Three hundred dollars is three hundred dollars. Nobody said how it was going to be paid."
Brad: "You're an asshole!"

I was trying hard not to busting out laughing, but like a bad case of diarrhea, I let loose. *Another creative bet by Ethan.* I didn't feel bad for Brad but I did feel bad for the poor individual at the bank who had to count every one of those 30,000 pennies. Meanwhile Brad was angry and dumbfounded. He just sat there on the couch like a kid who had just dropped his ice cream. There was nothing he could do. Brad ended up taking his three hundred dollar buckets home with him that night.

K- Korean strippers, black strippers, white strippers, Latin strippers; Ethan loved them all. His world revolved around them. After getting off work from the strip club, they would often come to Ethan's house because they knew they could make a little extra cash while having a good time. Every time I came to Ethan's house, he seemed to be accompanied by a stripper.

L- Lust was Ethan's biggest weakness and he knew it. He was a pussy fiend. The good news is that Ethan was not stingy with the strippers he knew. He would fly in strippers from all over the United States to entertain his houseguests.

M- My craziest memory of one of Ethan's parties involved of half-naked strippers. They were lined up inside of his house as you walked in. These women were ready to "service" all

of his party guests. These were not just average strippers; these were the crim de la crim, top of the line, thoroughbreds. Each was giving out party favors in the form of blowjobs. If you needed to relieve some stress, all you had to do was ask.

Ethan likened his strippers to different types of businesses. The strippers that liked to give it up for free, he referred to as non-profits and the for- profit strippers were like bill collector and required a method of payment. Cash on delivery. They were strictly in it for the dead presidents. Most of the for-profits would not even look your way unless the conversation started with Jackson, Hamilton, Franklin, and the like.

N- Non-Profit businesses were the partygoers' favorites. The non-profits didn't seem as money hungry as the for-profits and were often down to earth. Besides, who doesn't want something for free? Because of the high profile guests at Ethan's parties, non-profits would often get extremely generous tips and end up making more than the for-profits.

O- Orange Juice, Bacardi 151, Jamaican Rum, and White Rum all make up Ethan's favorite drink: the New Orleans Hurricane. During one his parties, Ethan had been drinking his Hurricane potion and was lit like Vegas strip at night. This caused him to start one of his crazy rants, while daring anyone to refute his claims. Liquid courage is a bitch.

Ethan, sitting on the couch and holding his drink, starts making absurd declarations while a topless Cuban stripper sits on his lap.

ETHAN: "There is nobody in this house that can fuck with me in basketball. I was all state all five years in high school. My crossover is like A.I. from back in the day and I have a better jump shot than Ray Allen."

Calling his bluff, I question him over the loud music.

ME: "Five years? Really? Get outta here! You can't go to high school for five years. It's not college. Now, I know you're lying."

ETHAN: "Well you know what I mean. It wasn't five years it was four but same thing. I was All-Florida. I should have played in the McDonald's All-American game. Had offers to almost every school in the nation."

Sarcastically, I agree with his claims.

ME: "I guess..."

Ethan got increasingly frustrated the more I doubted his claims. Meanwhile, some for-profits gathered around the couch like a campfire.

ETHAN: "They would refer to me as baby Jordan. Kobe and Lebron had nothing on me! The only reason I'm not in the NBA is because I decided to play football instead. Florida is known for recruiting top talent in football. We have the best football players in the nations."

Brad happened to be in the same room and jumped into the discussion.

> **BRAD:** "What are you guys fussing about?"
> **ME:** "His drunk-ass said that he was an all-state basketball player for five years...in high school! Then he says he can beat anyone in the house at a game of basketball."
> **ETHAN:** "Fucking right!"

Ethan takes another sip of his Hurricane. While still in a drunken stupor, Ethan walks over to the DJ booth and snatches the microphone, Ethan turns toward the DJ.

> **ETHAN:** "DJ, cut this shit down for a second."

The music gets lower and as well as everyone's voices.

> **ETHAN:** "To all my beautiful people here, I got something to say! *Shhhh.* Listen up. Whoever. I mean whoever. Well first of thank you for coming. What am I trying to say? Oh yeah. Whoooooever thinks they can beat me in a one-on-one basketball game, come up to the DJ Booth. Come to the DJ booth and I will beat your ass. Nobody can fuck with me."

Realizing Ethan is drunk, a few of the guests walk over and attempt to take the microphone from Ethan, but he guards the microphone as if he is protecting his life. He then speaks back into the microphone to make another point.

ETHAN: "Back up people. This is my mutha fuckin' house.
I do what the fuck I want. If it is my mutha fuckin' house then
this is my mutha mic. And if this is my mutha fuckin' mic then
I dictate the mutha fuckin' rules. And the rules say if anyone
wants some of me on the court right now. I'm placing bets! I
know I'm kinda drunk right now, but I will still hit a jump shot
in everyone's eye. I'm the man around this bitch!"

Ethan waits for a few seconds while trying to maintain his balance.
Nobody at the party takes his offer.

ETHAN: "That is what I mutha fuckin' thought. Ya'll are
some bitches! Let's keep this party going, drunk up my
beautiful people."

Ethan hands the mic back to the DJ. The DJ turns the music back
on and Ethan returns to his seat and tries to call me out.

ETHAN: "I see you didn't want none of this. Punk ass."

Brad still salty from his previous bet with Ethan leans over and tries
to entice me.

Brad "You better take him on his offer. If the tables were
turned, he would take advantage of you."

P-   Peer pressure will make you do things that you normally
     would not do. Ethan had just called me out and was testing
     my manhood. Additionally, Brad was encouraging me to take
     Ethan's offer. I turned to Ethan with a slight smirk on my face.

ME: "Do you have any basketball shorts?"

Like Al Pacino in the movie Scarface, Ethan swore he was the kingpin.

ETHAN: "You out of all people want to challenge me? You don't need shorts. Play with what you have on. I am about to beat you. Drunk and all! I've seen you play basketball and I was definitely not impressed."

Q- Questioning my level of basketball skills was the worst thing Ethan could have done. My pride will not allow me to get disrespected, even by a drunk friend.

ME: "You have yourself a bet! Now, what are we betting?"

Ethan pauses for a second and thinks. He looks up the topless Cuban still sitting on his lap.

R- Raising his eyebrows, he wages the bet.

ETHAN: "Winner walks away with his pride."
ME: "You got it! Where is the ball?"
ETHAN: "Not so fast."

ME: "I'm not putting any money on this game so that I can get an extra 30,000 pennies added to my name."
ETHAN: "No, No, No. The winner's prize stays the same. He walks away with his pride."
ME: "What about the loser?"

ETHAN: "Wes, I want you to meet Sapphire."

I reach out to shake Sapphire's hand while trying not to look at her perky DD breasts.

ETHAN: "Sapphire is currently wearing only a yellow thong. The loser, using only his mouth has to slide her thong all the way off."

S- Sapphire looks at me and then shrugs her shoulders, not objecting to what Ethan had just proposed.

ME: "No problem, you are just giving me incentive to lose the game..."
ETHAN: "...Again, not so fast. See, that is your problem. You are always trying to jump ahead of what the fuck I'm trying to tell you."
ME: "Sorry, go ahead."
ETHAN: "Fuck, let me gather my thoughts. You are over here interrupting me and shit. OK, after you slide her panties off while using your mouth, the loser has to eat her out while reciting the ABC's...backwards. That's right backwards, like reverse. As in, the opposite of forward. And...the winner gets to tape it on video. That way when people ask about your basketball game we will know it is pussy. And you are what you eat."

T- Traumatized and shocked about what just came out of the belligerent drunk's mouth, I accepted. *Another creative bet by*

Ethan. With all the people at the party, I was determined not to lose. We headed out to the backyard where there was a full size basketball court. Ethan instructed Brad to grab a ball and a video camera to tape the game.

While holding the ball at the top of the key, Ethan explained the rules.

ETHAN: "I have the ball first since this is my court. We will play till 5, straight up. Call your own fouls and anything behind the three-point line is still only counted as 1 point. Any questions?"

Mockingly I dared him to do the unthinkable.

ME: "Yeah, you think that you can hit that shot over me?"

Ethan heaves the ball from the top of the three-point line. SWISH. Ethan gives me the birdie while updating me with the score.

ETHAN: "One for me and a goose egg for you. Any other questions?"

Ethan takes the ball starts to dribble, crosses over to the left, then to the right. As I cut off his pathway to the hoop, he pulls up from the wing for a jump shot.

ETHAN: "Bank."

The ball hits the backboard and goes in.

ME: "Son of a bitch!"

Ethan raises both his hands in the air signifying to the crowd who the man is.

ETHAN: "I hope you're hungry, cause you have a lot of pussy to eat! I told you nobody could fuck with me."

Gaining more and more confidence Ethan gets even louder.

ETHAN: "Two for me and none for you. Hey, this kinda sounds like our sex lives. I am scoring two at a time while you aren't gettin' any."

Hearing all of the commotion, a majority of the partygoers have now made their way outside to the basketball court. Even the DJ announces the game over the microphone.

DJ: "For those that want to check out some more action, there is heated basketball game going on between Ethan and one of his compadres."

Ethan has now started to sober up, yet still determined to beat me. One of the onlookers is Sapphire. She sits on a nearby ledge eagerly waiting for the game to be finished. Out of all of us, Sapphire was making out like a bandit. Regardless of the outcome in this game, she was about to get her cookie eaten like a Nutter Butter.

U- Unsuccessful thus far at scoring any points, I start to look for ways to find a chink in Ethan's armor.

Ethan takes the ball from the top of the key and bounces it to me.

ETHAN: "Check."

I bounce it back to him. Ethan starts his trash talking again.

ETHAN: "You see all those people out here watching me? They know me as Magic because they are just like you, always on my Johnson. They know talent when they see it, and right now that is all they see."

Ethan tries to repeat the same move on me and dribbles to the left. He then tries to cross over to the right.

V- Violently, I move my hand in the ball's pathway and snatch it. The crowd cheers.

ME: "Where are you going Magic? Took that from you like a rabbit out of a hat."

Next, I dribble the ball down in the paint and now have him posted up.

ME: "This is a more realistic look at our sex lives: You trying to score and me snatching what you thought you had."

The voices from the crowd can be heard with sprinkles of *oohs* and *ahhs* as we biker back and forth.

While having my back to the basket, I fake left then fake right. I turn around and hit a fade away jumper.

ME: "2-1"

Soon as I get the ball back at the top of the key, I jab step and shoot. Brick. I race past Ethan and grab my own rebound and put it back in the basket, 2-2.

A frustrated Ethan plays his tightest defense on me this time. I fake left and he over plays my left side. I change direction and dribble to the right and head toward the basket. Amazingly, he recovers and, as I come closer to the basket, I stop and give a hard pump fake. He pops up like popcorn in an attempt to block my shot. I put the ball in for an easy point as he comes down from horribly timed jump. Wes-3, Ethan-2.

ETHAN: "What the fuck? You keep getting these lucky shots."
ME: "Don't worry about my game; just worry about what you have to do, Mr. Magic Johnson."

This time, as I hold the ball at the top of the key, Ethan lets me blow past him in an attempt to bait me to the basket so he can block my shot. As I go up for what I think is an easy lay-up, he blocks my shot so hard it heads straight out of bounds. The crown erupts and Ethan poses a question for the crowd.

ETHAN: "Does anyone know what zip code where that ball landed in?"

One of the for-profit bystanders retrieves the ball and throws it back on the court. I take the ball from the top of the key. Ethan tries to get me to take a long shot.

ETHAN: "If you're as good as you say you are, then you will hit that shot."

I don't respond.

I act like I am going to attempt the shot. Eagerly, Ethan jumps the gun anticipating that I will concede to his challenge. I go to shoot, however, Ethan lands on me and I can't even get my shot off.

ME: "Foul! I never said I was good, just better than you."

Ethan grabs the ball and slaps it in frustration of his recently committed foul. He hands the ball to me and we are back in action. I can sense that Ethan is starting to panic because he feels as though the game is out of his control.

I back him down in the paint again. Impatient, Ethan goes in for the steal and I simultaneously reverse spin toward the basketball for another easy point. The score is now 4-2.

Brad shouts out from amongst the onlookers.

BRAD: "Put him out of his misery! He was never *all state*. He was just all-bullshit."

This time, I change up my strategy and decide to hit the long shot. I shoot and miss. Like Déjà vu, I grab my own rebound once again and put the ball in.

W- Winning never felt so great.

> **ME:** "That's game. 5-2! Wow, what a coincidence, you actually got beat like Sapphire's height. She *is* around 5'2" wouldn't you say? Hope you saved room for dessert."

The drunken party guests clap and cheer as if they had just witnessed Game seven of the NBA finals. I walked off the court and waived to the fans to show my appreciation. Next, I picked up a folding chair and place it at half court.

> **ME:** "Oh, Ethan. It's dinner time!"

Brad hands me the video camera and I start recording. Brad talks to the camera as if he is a sideline reporter.

> **BRAD:** "We are here live at Ethan court, where we have just witnessed a lopsided victory by Wes over the ever-so struggling Ethan. Ethan was ahead by two points but Wes came back in a miraculous 5 unanswered point comeback. Stay tuned for the post game show where we will broadcast Ethan eating his post-game meal. I am Brad McKinney reporting live back to you, Wes."

Ethan walked towards the chair at half court where a topless Sapphire was now standing. Being a good sport, Ethan approached Sapphire and got on his knees. Ethan began sliding down her yellow thong inch by inch from her left hip while only using his teeth.

Once he reached as far as he could from the left, he repeated the same process on the right hip, in front of all the perverted onlookers. He slid her thong to the ground, exposing her clean-shaved pussycat. Brad then started giving both Ethan and Sapphire directions.

BRAD: "OK, sit your ass on this chair, Ms. Sapphire, so Ethan can eat his dinner."

Sapphire sat down in the chair spread eagle and encouraged Ethan in her Spanish accent.

SAPPHIRE: "Come on, big boy!"

Ethan approached the pussy face first with his hands behind his back and started eating like a ravishing wolf.

BRAD: "Whoa, slow down there tiger. The pussy is not going anywhere. Is that how you eat your food at the dinner table?"

X- XXX at its best. In front of the whole party, I was on a basketball court filming Ethan eating a stripper's apple pie with Brad reporting on the action. Ethan was in his own world and focused on his task. I suddenly stopped him.

ME: "Wait, wait, and wait. I don't hear anything. Since I don't hear anything, I am feeling extremely illiterate right now because somebody has not taught me my ABC's. So, Ethan if you will please."

Brad started to color commentate again.

> **BRAD:** "Folks you are about to witness the good ol'
> alphabet song from our Florida all-State basketball player.
> ETHAN! While he tries to make this pussy cum like a
> hurricane. Give it up ladies and gentleman while Ethan
> attempts to sing the alphabet song."

Ethan takes another muff dive and eats away. He begins the ABC
song with the worst lisp in the world.

> **ETHAN:** "A, Thee(*B*), she(*C*), thee(*D*), E, S(*F*), thee(*G*),
> eight(*H*), I, They(*J*)--"
> **ME:** "Hold on, stop! This is not was not what we agreed
> to! What's wrong? Cat got your tongue? I need to hear
> the alphabet *backwards*!"
> **ETHAN:** "I'm trying, okay."
> **ME:** "Try harder; I'm really trying to know my ABC's or
> better yet my CBA's. You may want to move the yellow
> thongs from where you are kneeling so they don't get in
> the way while you are working down there. Alright, let's
> go, from the top."

Ethan rolled his eyes and I once again started rolling the videotape.

> **ETHAN:** "Thee (*Z*), eye(*Y*), S(*X*)--"

While I was filming Ethan eating Sapphire's apple pie, Brad used his
best impression of the Crocodile Hunter to throw in his two cents.

BRAD: "Here we have the wet pussycat hailing all the way from Chicago. Isn't she a beauty? Now if you look really close, you can see a different kind of species. He is from the looser species. Now folks, this species tends to bite off more than they can chew. Would you look at the technique he is using? He is using the muscles in his tongue to try and tame the wet pussycat. Oh and you hear that? Come closer. It sounds like he is trying to recite the alphabet. In actuality, that is his pathetic mating call."

Y- Yellow panties being slid off and the Alphabet song being sung backwards at center court in front of the many onlookers, Ethan had finally met his match regarding outlandish bets. Ethan finally finished the rest of the alphabet all the way up through A.

After the alphabet, we all went back to parying as if nothing ever happened. Ethan was such a great sport that he played the video on his big screen in his living room and made the party that much more enjoyable. The ABC event caused Sapphire to receive a lot of generous tips. I may not be the best basketball player in the world but I was good enough to win one of my most daring bets, compliments of Ethan. The good thing about the whole situation was that from...

Z- Z thru A and from A thru Z, I now knew my ABC's.

Chapter 10

Me Gusta, Me Gusta...
No Me Gusta

When I was living in Washington, DC, my friends and I spent a weekend in Philadelphia. Philly is about a two hour ride from Washington, DC. While out in Philly, I met Leticia in a salsa club. I never imagined it would amount to anything nor did I think that I would ever see her again. Regardless, we still maintained contact in the latter weeks upon me leaving Philly.

One weekend, Leticia decides to make a trip down to DC and spend the weekend with me. She buys a ticket and takes the Amtrak from Philly to DC. A few of her friends had told her about this night-club called Love and she was set on going there once she arrived.

Since I knew Leticia was on her way down from Philly, I dialed up Parker. Parker as mentioned in How I Made Love To A Porn Star was like my life coach. I would call him whenever I needed some advice on women. Sometimes he gave great advice, other times his advice was horrible. He was more inconsistent at giving solutions than a political candidate.

ME: "Hey Parker, remember the Columbian I was telling you about? Well she is coming to see me tonight."

PARKER: "The hot chick from Philadelphia?"

ME: "Yeah. When she gets in this evening we are supposed to go out to a club. Any suggestions on what to order a gorgeous Columbian once we get to the bar?"

PARKER: "I have to words for you: *patron* and *pineapple*. A few shots of that and she will be good to go."

ME: "Patron and pineapple, huh?"

PARKER: "Trust me on this dude. She won't even taste the patron. It goes down nice and easy. By the time you get to your place, she will be the one going down nice and easy...on your pineapple. Let me know how it goes."

After speaking with Parker, I decide to give his strategy a try. When she finally arrives in DC we head over to my place and get ready. Soon after, we head out to Love nightclub. After bypassing security we head in to party. Love was one of the biggest clubs that I had ever been to. This club was four stories high with a different DJ on each floor.

Leticia makes a B-line to the dance floor. Next, she starts to dance and begins moving her hips to the music like only a Latina can. I start to get infatuated by this fine thing moving in front of me. As the music blasts over the speakers and the club lights bounce off of this beauty, I come to a realization. I am lust struck.

Parker's voice echoes throughout my head. "Patron and pineapple." I excuse myself from the dance floor and head to the bar. I order a Patron and pineapple for Leticia and straight cranberry juice for myself. I make it back to the dance floor and hand her the drink.

LETICIA: "Gracias."

She takes her first sip and lights up.

LETICIA: "Mmm. Que es esto?"

Proud of myself for passing beginner Spanish in high school, I confidently let her know that I understood what the fuck she just said to me.

ME: "It's Patron and pineapple."
LETICIA: "Me gusta!"

Next, I try to impress her by showing her how diverse I am with my language skills. I then proceed to mix up my languages like a DJ on some turntables.

ME: "Yeah, me gusta too... tambien."

Bilingualism at its best.

We continued to dance the night away. Trying to keep up with Leticia on the dance floor was one of the best workouts of my life. I must have burned every calorie that my body had taken in the past week. The only breaks that I took were frequent trips back to the bar. A few drinks later, I could tell that Parker knew what he was talking about. Leticia was getting tipsy and the Patron and pineapple juice was working.

LETICIA: "I'm getting kind of tired. How much longer do you want to stay?"

ME: "I'm ready to go, but I'm a little hungry. Would you mind stopping to get something to eat on the way back?"
LETICIA: "No, not at all. I'm not going to eat; I ate right before I got on the train."

We leave the club and I decide to get some of America's best gourmet food. McDonald's. Who wouldn't want a McChicken Sandwich's mystery meat at 1 am? The McChicken Sandwich tastes like it could be made from rubber. That meat can't be chicken.

As we walk in to McDonald's I place my order for the Mc-Chicken sandwich. I notice that Leticia may have had one too many Patron and pineapples. She is looking off into space, babbling at the mouth and blowing spit bubbles. Like a negligent doctor, I have over prescribed. This calls for a slight detour in my plans. My mission, now, is to get her somewhat sober. If she passes out then I won't' be able to get my McRib licked on.

I scarf down my meal and we head back to my place. When we walk into my house it felt like a McFlurry so I had to turn the heat on so it would get warm like a McSkillet. We jump in my bed under the covers like couple of McWraps. While between the sheets, we get our McFrench on. She is not nearly as drunk as she was earlier. I am now in it to win it. Parker's advice was spot on.

Having this woman in my bed only makes me feel like a Big-Mac. I take her shirt and bra off and now I am sucking on her firm McGriddles. Her cup size had to be at a least McDouble D. I unbuckle her jeans and start feeling on her wet Egg McMuffin. It just makes me want to quarter and pound her.

LETICIA: "Papi, lay on your back."

I roll over and she straddles my Big N' Tasty. She reciprocates what I did for her and removes my clothes.

Next, she heads down and starts to lick my Chicken McNuggets.

LETICIA: "Te gusta?"
ME: "Si mami, me gusta. Keep going!"

After licking my McNuggets, she moves toward my McRib. She gets really into it and starts to moan. I start to moan as well. In a matter of hours, she went from being the top 5 hottest women in the club to being top five best blowjobs I have ever had. In between slurps and gags on my McRib, she was talking to dirty to me in Spanish. Then she popped up to check my approval.

LETICIA: "You like?"

This blowjob was a masterpiece.

ME: "Yeah, mami. Keep going; don't stop."

She went back to work. This time was even better than before. I felt a tingling coming on as if I was about to shoot my McCafe' milkshake, which got me talking dirty.

ME: "Yeah, baby, suck on it real good. Just like that. Me gusta, me gusta!"

Then she suddenly stopped. There were no more slurping sounds, no gagging sounds, and no more sucking. Just dead silence. Uh oh, I think I may have offended her.

ME: "Is it something I said?"

No response. I lifted my head up off of the pillow and take a quick peek downtown. She was motionless.

ME: "Um, hello?"

Still no response.

ME: "Leticia, you awake? Leticia?"

Leticia started moving again.

LETICIA: "Sorry about that."

As she came back to life, she noticed my McRib was against her cheek. She turned and started sucking my McRib again.

She was a winner. The things she was doing couldn't be taught; she had natural talent. In her Spanish accent she started making demands.

LETICIA: "Talk to me baby. Tell me how much you like it."
ME: "Me gusta, me gusta! Ohhh...me gusta!"
LETICIA: "Cum for me papi."

I couldn't hold it anymore. She was so good that I was not concerned if I was unable to put my McSausage in her McBiscuit. I was about to erupt like a volcano as I continued to encourage her. But somehow, something went wrong.

> **ME:** "Si, me gusta, me gusta...NO ME GUSTA!!!"

All the dick sucking came to an end, right when I was about to make a milkshake. She lay there motionless. I started to scold her like a puppy in obedience training.

> **ME:** "What the—aww hell no! No me gusta Leticia! No me gusta. Wake up! No, no, no. This is not happening to me right now."

Frustrated, I shook the shit out of Leticia. She didn't even respond. I slapped her as if she were dead batteries in a TV remote in an attempt to revive her.

> **ME:** "Wake up mamcita, wake up!"

I then hear her make a noise. Yes! A sign of life. The sound starts off very low and then rumbles and gradually gets louder. She lets out a fart so loud it would have made Walter the farting dog proud.

> **ME:** "Oh no, me gusta."

I give her another desperate shake. She lays there motionless. Then she starts snoring like a bear in hibernation. I take a deep breath

and lay in the bed sexually frustrated. Not to mention, my McRib felt neglected and teased from being on the receiving end of the best job the century had to offer.

I had run out of options. I just sat in bed looking at the ceiling. I then heard Parker's voice reminding me how I got into this ugly predicament. "Patron and pineapple." I knew I shouldn't have listened to Parker. He gets me into trouble every time.

At this point I just wanted to go to sleep. However, it was impossible because I noticed a sharp pain coming from my Big N' Tasty area. All of a sudden my McNuggets were internally on fire. It felt as if Jackie Chan had given them a thousand kung fu kicks. I moved Leticia off of me, got out of the bed and walked toward my cell phone on the other side of the room, which was on my desk. The first person I thought of calling was Parker so that I could cuss him out for ruining my night. He answered on the first ring.

PARKER: "Why are you calling me? Shouldn't you be banging that Columbian chick right now?"
ME: "She is passed out in my bed at the moment, Mr. Patron and pineapple."
PARKER: "Nice! Was I right or was I right?"
ME: "Hell no, you weren't right! I didn't even get a chance to bang her. She passed out as she was giving me head."
PARKER: "No freakin' way dude! That's awesome."
ME: "The hell it is. I barely made it past first base. Let alone, close to hitting a home run. But that is beside the point. Listen, I am in excruciating pain! My gonads hurt like a son of a bitch."
PARKER: "Whoa! You have problems."

ME: "Yeah I do. What is going on with my nuts?"

PARKER: "You've got blue balls dude."

ME: "Blue balls?"

PARKER: "Tell me you've heard of blue balls."

ME: "I have, I just thought that was an urban legend. Never thought that really happened. What do I do? Should I ice them?"

PARKER: "No way. There is only one remedy for blue balls. You have to go to the bathroom and rub one out. If you don't, you will have unbearable pain all night. Here is a suggestion. Wake her up and have her finish the BJ."

ME: "I tried that already. I've tried everything. She won't wake up. She is doing everything else but waking up. She keeps farting and snoring, as if they go hand in hand."

PARKER: "Just chalk it up then and rub one out. Anyway I have this girl coming over right now I have to get going."

I hang up the phone with Parker, set the phone down and head back over to a passed out Leticia.

ME: "Wake up! **Please** wake up!"

Once again, she lets out a snore. By now she has drooled all over my pillow like a St. Bernard. I eventually give up waking this Columbian beauty. No me gusta. It went from bad to worse in a hurry. I finally came to the realization that choking my McChicken was going to be my best option. I was in so much pain. I made my way down the hall towards the bathroom with my head down, my dick up and my balls en fuego.

Patron and pineapple ruined my whole night. But wait, the night was not completely over. I had a fine Latina in my bedroom and I had a hard McRib. Was it my fault that she couldn't hold her liquor and passed out while giving me a blowjob? No. Well, sort of but who is really keeping track.

Like a professional criminal I began to plan out the perfect crime scene and method of attack. I can frame the perfect blow-job just like the perfect murder. For all I know, Leticia will only remember that right before she passed out; she was slurping my McRib, therefore, she doesn't know how it ended. If I can make it look like I came right before she passed out, then I will be in good shape. I rushed back into the bedroom and turned the lights on.

Next, I stood over the edge of the bed where she was passed out while simultaneously looking at her hotcakes. I started choking my McChicken to ease the pain in my huevos. She barely moved a muscle. I erupted and shot my milkshake, which traveled in the shape of a golden arch. My Filet-O-Fish tartar sauce ends up landing all over her hair. It looked as if someone dumped a Kiddie Cone on her.

Fucked up, I know but I was just lending her a helping hand. Who else was there to assist what she had started? Soon after, the pain in my McNuggets subsided and eventually went away. I guess Parker was right after all.

I finally was able to go to sleep that night. I woke up the next morning and Leticia was finally alive. Leticia's memory was a little fuzzy regarding the previous night's events, which was natural.

LETICIA: "What happened last night?"

ME: "To make a long story short, after the club, we got something to eat at McDonald's. We came back to my place and you started blowing my brains out. As I was about to cum, you passed out on me. I couldn't wake you up. I ended up getting blue balls so I started to go to the bathroom to finish myself but instead I returned to the room and came in your hair."

LETICIA: "You did what? You came in my hair?"

Ashamed of what I did, I hung my head and answered truthfully.

ME: "I did."

LETICIA: "Oh no, Papi... Me gusta!"

Leticia and I headed back to my bathroom and got in the shower. While in the shower, she even went back down on my Big and Tasty and I was able to later put it in her hotcakes. This time I was blue ball free when it was all said and done. Me gusta, me gusta.

Chapter 11

The Three Wheel Motion

Hitting the three wheel motion is a phrase used by low-rider enthusiasts to describe when an automobile with hydraulics installed, drives on three wheels. The term was made famous during the 90s when Ice Cube used it in his song. Furthermore, it describes a new sex position that I invented. It all started in the Northwest.

Cidric was a boxer that I met while out in Seattle, Washington. Cidric was just starting his professional fighting career and invited me out to celebrate one of his recent victories. We decided to head over to BelltownBilliards (BB), which was primarily a pool hall. However, during certain nights of the week, BB would turn into a nightclub.

We decided to head over to BB one night with two main objectives:

1) Find some ass to crush
2) Crush that ass.

Once we entered BB, the dance floor was like a coffee stand, it was packed with Seattle's Best. There was black coffee, a few mochas, but primarily lattes. There was one particular latte that caught my eye from across the room.

Since there were so many people in the club it was hard to get a really good look at her. My view while looking at her was going in and out like a strobe light. However, that didn't stop me from pointing her out to Cidric as potential ass.

ME: "What do you think about that one over there in the red?"
CIDRIC: "You talking about the tall blonde velour suit?"
ME: "That's her."
CIDRIC: "She is the finest thing in here, hands down! Go ahead and swing away my friend; swing away."

I had just completed the first objective: finding ass to crush.

I made my way through the crowd until I was face to face with the blonde bombshell. Initially, Cidric stayed behind but as soon as he saw how attractive her friends were, he immediately made his way over. Cidric had now completed the first objective as well.

After a brief introduction, the blonde revealed to us that her name was Rae and attended the University of Washington along with her friends. After some more small talk, I pulled Rae aside so I could have a one on one conversation with her and work on objective number two.

ME: "What are ya'll doing after you leave here?"
RAE: "I'm not sure. I am a little buzzed right now but we will probably head back to my place and keep on drinking throughout the night. I just had a midterm today and we decided to come out and celebrate."
ME: "How do you think you did?"

RAE: "Who knows? I don't even want to think about that right now. Can I tell you something?"
ME: "Be my guest"
RAE: "I think you are the hottest guy in here."
ME: "Funny you say that because earlier Cidric and I both voted the woman with the red velour suit was the finest girl at this club tonight."

This caused her to get all gitty. I was just hoping that she would gitty up on my dick. While laying the foundation for objective number two, I was simultaneously receiving envious looks from all the men in the club who wanted to talk to her but were too intimidated. It was apparent; I knew I had a winner. Rae was friendly, tall, and every guy's dream. The woman seemed flawless.

Although I was showing great signs of progress, my wingman was not so fortunate. It was clear that none of Rae's three friends were interested in Cidric. Cidric stood there like an unvaccinated kid; he had no shot. I refused to leave my wingman out in the cold so I wrapped things up with Rae and got her number in hopes of seeing her later that night. Next, Cidric and I did like a banana and split.

We took our game elsewhere and made our rounds throughout the club. I got greedy and must have thought I was at the rodeo because I was trying to round up every woman in the club. I ended up getting a few numbers but didn't spend a significant time getting to know them. They were just numbers, nothing more. I was feeling like a kid in a candy store because I couldn't decide on what type of woman I wanted to take home. Consequently, my indecisiveness proved to be detrimental.

The time for rounding up as many women as I could have expired. I had lost track of time, the DJ had just turned the music off and the club was closing. I was like an Asian women looking at herself in the mirror before she heads out; I realized I had no ass. Obtaining objective number two seemed more and more bleak as Cidric and I walked back to the car.

There is always hope when it comes to women, however, and sometimes you just have to play the numbers. I decided to implement Plan B and sent out a mass "I want to see you tonight" text message to all five women whom I had got a number from that night. The good news is that all five responded back to me. The bad news is that those responses consisted of:

1) Sorry, I'm not like that
2) I can't. I have work in the morning
3) Richard, is this your cell?
4) Why are you texting my girlfriend?
5) I have class early in the morning, but I can hangout for drinks tomorrow at happy hour.

Zero out of five. Those were definitely not Derek Jeter numbers. I decided to respond back to text message five because it happened to be Rae. We set up a time to meet at a local pub the following evening. At least the whole night wasn't a waste. The thought of Rae's back potentially being plastered on my mattress gave me a glimmer of hope. The next day, right before we were supposed to meet, Rae called to confirm that I was coming.

RAE: "Hey, I'm just making sure you know where you're going."

ME: "Yeah, I got it plugged in my navigation."

RAE: "Do you remember what I look like?"

ME: "Of course. I just saw you last night."

RAE: "True, but I wasn't sure if you were drunk or not."

ME: "Who could forget the tall blonde in the velour suit?"

RAE: "There is something I need to tell you before you get here."

ME: "Yeah? What is it?"

RAE: "Well, um… I don't think that you will recognize me when you get here."

ME: "What do you mean?"

In the back of my mind, I was thinking that I might have picked up a he-she. At this point, clarity was a priority.

ME: "You're not a dude are you?"

RAE: "Ha! No, I am very much a woman."

ME: "So you're not a chick –with-a-dick or nothing crazy like that right? Cause I don't get down like that at all. I'm not into all that freaky deaky shit. I don't try to go down different roads, I stay right on Pussy Avenue."

RAE: "Relax; you will see when you get here."

After hanging up the phone I felt like a child raised by a same-sex couple. Confused, looking for answers, and wondering what the hell was going on. I called Cidric to see if he could shed light on the situation.

ME: "You remember the blonde from last night?"

CIDRIC: "Yeah, the tall one in the red."

ME: "Well I am on my way to meet up with her and I was wondering if you noticed anything different about her. She told me that I probably wouldn't recognize her when I saw her. She wasn't wearing a turtleneck. Did you see an Adam's apple or anything?"

CIDRIC: "She seemed pretty normal to me. I bet she just did something to her hair like cut it or dyed it a different color."

ME: "I guess you're right, I think I'm overreacting. She just seemed too good to be true."

I eventually arrived at the pub. It was full of University of Washington students getting boozed off of dollar beers. As I stood near the front doorway of the pub, I felt a tap on side of my shoulder. As I turned to my right to see who it was, I noticed Rae smiling at me. I clearly recognized her and it seemed like there was nothing different about her. She had the same pretty smile, same hair length, same blond hair, and actually looked better than how I remembered her.

ME: "Hey Rae! Well, I must say, you look great. Why did you say that I wouldn't recognize you? You look the same as you did last night. What changed?"

Rae didn't say anything and shrugged her shoulders. There was something that she was hiding from me but I couldn't put my finger on it. Instead of wasting time figuring it out, I let it go.

ME: "Give me a hug and let's get this party started."

I reached out with both of my arms to give Rae a big bear hug. She reciprocated the gesture with a half-ass one-arm hug. Let me rewind that. She reciprocated with a one-arm hug. At that point, everything came together like two nymphos having sex. Rae only had one arm. She had a full right arm but her left arm was cut off at the elbow joint.

I tried to play it off and act like I didn't notice it. I'm sure my face said it all. I was horrified at first but then I got to thinking to myself. If one monkey don't stop no show, then one arm won't stop a hoe. She will just bring a whole new meaning to the phrase, *look ma no hands.*

I couldn't understand how I failed to notice her arm the night before last. Certain things people never fail to notice; such as coming face to face with a six-ton elephant, having the runs when eating mystery meat at the Chinese buffet, and beautiful women with one arm. Regardless of this new discovery, I was still determined to crush Rae's ass. Women like this don't come around like this very often.

We hung out for a few more hours at the bar and after a few drinks; she was good to go like a green light. She started to loosen up which also caused me to loosen up and blurt out a question that could have been saved for another time.

ME: "What the hell happened to your arm?"
RAE: "Excuse me?"
ME: "Well, I mean it's not there."
RAE: "No shit. When I was younger I had an accident and they had to remove it. But that hasn't stopped me from living life like I should. I can do everything else a person with two arms can do except climb on the monkey bars."

As long as a woman knows how to lick it like a lollipop, that's all that matters to me.

> ME: "Interesting. Well at least you don't let that limit you from doing what you want, kinda like me."
> RAE: "Like you? Oh is that right? Explain."
> ME: "A girl with two arms sitting at the bar with me would want to do me. Just because you don't have two arms shouldn't prevent you from doing me. Comprende?"
> RAE: "Oh, I comprende. You're a guy who knows what he wants and is not afraid to voice it. I like that. You want to leave this place, and hang out at my spot for a bit?"
> ME: "Sure."
> RAE: "I live right around the corner. You can follow me."
> ME: "Your car isn't stick is it?"
> RAE: "I see you have jokes. We'll see who is making jokes when we get to my place."

I took Rae's words as an invitation to lend her my third arm.

Once we arrived at her place, I sat down at her kitchen table contemplating my next move. I didn't have to think too long because she came over to where I was sitting and straddled me.

> RAE: "So... you were questioning my ability to drive stick?"
> ME: "I was. I still am."

Rae slowly grinded on my lap in a back and forth motion. Then she sped up real fast and started moving like U-Haul. I started to

sink deeper in the chair like a low-rider. Little did I know Rae was a freak, I'm talking stone cold like Steve Austin.

With a girl like Rae, I really wondered how many miles she had on her speedometer. She was very attractive but she was like a Barbie doll at a day care center, she was missing a few parts. How many guys were able to look past that? I know I could.

Meanwhile, she continued riding me with my jeans on. Next, she started bouncing her bumper up and down in my lap. She briefly stopped to check on her passenger.

RAE: "How is that for driving stick?"
ME: "That was great... but that wasn't reality. That was like driving stick in a video game. It was fun, exciting, but not even close to the real thing."
RAE: "I was just giving you a preview of my driving skills."

Rae then started to rev my engine up. She began nibbling me on my neck and tonguing my front grille. I reached for her front airbags and dropped her top. She had the perfect pair of airbags.

ME: "You have the most perfect pair of tits I ever seen."
RAE: "Yeah everyone asks me who my doctor is, but they are real."

I guess the compliment made her even hornier. She then reached down with her one arm and unbuckled my serpentine belt. Next, she reached in and pulled out my drive shaft. She started pulling it back and forth like a stuck seatbelt in an '85 Cutlass. She still had her skirt on so I reached for her center console to slide her

panties to the side. When my hand got to her center console, it was flooded and her panties were nonexistent.

RAE: "As you can tell... I'm ready to test drive your stick."
ME: "Be my guess Danica Patrick."

Rae put my drive shaft in her flooded center console and started hitting switches on it. She was moving up and down, back and forth. Rae was about to make me blow a gasket. I lifted her off of me, turned her around and lifted up her skirt.

I was hesitant about getting behind her in the driver's seat because I was not sure if her one arm would mess with the suspension in her pussy. I figured it couldn't hurt to try. So like a Mexican in a maximum-security prison, I took a stab.

I bent her over so that she was on all fours threes and started giving it to her. I was essentially hitting the three-wheel motion. Three wheels were making contact with the ground while I was driving just like the low-riders do. I reached over with my hand and gave myself a pat on the back. I had just invented a new sex position: the three wheel motion.

Meanwhile, she started throwing her bumper back at me. We both wanted control of the steering wheel and were trying to outdo one another. However, our drive was suddenly cut short because we both ran out of gas. Rae could barely talk and was out of breath.

RAE: "Tired already?"

Attempting to toot my own horn, I lied.

ME: "Tired? I'm just getting started."

RAE: "Then why did you stop?"

ME: "You looked like you needed a break."

RAE: "Don't blame that on me. I'll let you know when I need you to stop."

It's amazing what a ten-second break will do in the middle of a sex session. My battery had recharged and I was back to hitting the three wheel motion. A few strokes later, I heard myself rumbling like a '64 Chevy with a supercharged engine. You guessed it; she made me spill all of my power steering fluid.

When it was all said and done, the kitchen was like a traffic accident. Objects were turned over, there were fluids on the ground and there were two witnesses who were able testify as to what they had just seen.

ME: "Wow that was great. I will doubt your driving abilities again."

RAE: "Glad you liked it."

Rae's phone started vibrating on the kitchen counter. She ran over and excitingly answered it.

RAE: "Hey! Yeah, I'm just getting in from the bar... uh huh... uh huh. Yeah, sure. Okay. I love you too."

Trying to be funny, I jokingly made a comment.

ME: "Was that a worried father checking on his baby girl?"

RAE: "No, that was my boyfriend, and you have to leave because he is on his way over here."

ME: "You never told me you had a boyfriend."

RAE: "You never asked... If you would have asked then I would have told you."

ME: "But what did we just do? What was that?"

RAE: "To put it bluntly we just fucked. But if you don't leave now then I'm going to be fucked if my boyfriend catches you over here."

I left Rae's place with my tail between my legs and had to take the walk of shame out of her place.

When I got to my car my phone rang. Regretfully, I picked up.

CIDRIC: "How did it go?"

ME: "I have the craziest story for you-"

CIDRIC: "Before you tell me, was I right about you not being able to recognize her because she dyed her hair?"

ME: "Negative. You know how those low-riders can hit the three wheel motion..."

I explained the rest of the story to Cidric and he was tickled to death. Once the weekend arrived, Cidric decided to meet up at the mall.

CIDRIC: "Have you talked to ARM and Hammer lately? Personally, I think that you should stay away from girls like Rae because they are *ARM*ed and dangerous."

ME: "Very funny."

CIDRIC: "Is a woman like that even eligible for the ARMed Forces? I mean if she was in the ARMy, wouldn't that make her an ARMy of one?"

ME: "Laugh all you want. One arm and all, she still looked better than any girl I have ever seen you with. Can you at least ease up on all the jokes?"

CIDRIC: "You're right. I'm sorry, No more jokes. I just need to pick up a shirt anyway."

ME: "Alright, where are we headed?"

CIDRIC: "ARMani Exchange."

Chapter 12

Wash Your Hands
Before You Eat

Life lessons are meant to be just that: lessons that stays with you throughout your lifetime. So when your parents tell you to wash your hands before you eat, you should always adhere to their advice. Like a student from the school of hard knocks, I learned that lesson the hard way.

One weekend, my friend Gus invited me to a baseball tournament at Chico State where he was coaching. Chico State is known for being a campus full of panty raids, rowdiness and a place where alcohol consumption is a favorite past time. Year after year, Playboy ranks Chico State as a top party school. Hundreds of funny sex stories occur every week and minewas no different.

When we arrived at Chico State, we decide to take a stroll through the campus. We happened to run into these two girls who were identical twins as well as roommates, Addison and Ava. Gus and I made some preliminary observations and discussed them amongst each other.

ME: "Those twins have twins!"
GUS: "And those asses are ass-tronomical! When did they start making jeans big enough to fit all that ass?"

ME: "I don't know, but we might as well go find out."

Gus and I went over and introduced ourselves. Ava and Addison were not the brightest students in the world and must have gotten admitted to college on looks alone. We weren't really interested in their brainpower, though, we were just interested in the power they had when giving brains. We briefly got to know them and the rest was history. Needless to say, they invited us over to their place that evening to hangout.

We got to Addison and Ava's two-bedroom apartment, and they already had dinner for us cooking in the oven.

AVA: "Make yourselves at home and have a seat on the couch."
ADDISON: "I hope you guys are hungry. I cooked my special lasagna. It's a family recipe passed down forever from generation to generation."
ME: "I'm starving."
GUS: "I wouldn't mind having some as well."
AVA: "Great! Also, once we finish dinner, I'm going to throw some brownies in the oven...also a family recipe."
ME: "Looks like we're dealing with a family affair tonight."

Addison got up, headed to the kitchen and took the lasagna out of the oven. Ava followed Addison's lead and fixed us all plates of food. We ate and laughed while watching an old cowboy movie on TBS. Between the big plate of lasagna and the movie on television, I dozed off.

I wasn't sure how long I had been asleep but I was awoken by the rhythmic sounds of a headboard banging against the wall in the

next room. I was still trying to shake the cobwebs off when realized I was on the couch alone.

I quickly came to the realization that Gus was having an intense cardio session with one of the twins in the next room but I had no idea with which one. *Was it Ava or Addison?*

From where I was sitting on the couch, I could see that one bedroom door happened to be wide open with the light on. I could hear movement in the open bedroom so I knew one of the twins was back there and all alone. Throughout my life experiences, I've come to know that siblings are very competitive and I knew whichever twin was in the backroom was feeling left out. I was determined to create a little bit of a sibling rivalry. I couldn't let Gus and whichever twin he was sexing outperform the remaining twin and me.

Over the years, I have learned that there are two basic rules which can often be applied to life:

RULE 1) Some people do dumb things.

RULE 2) Sometimes those dumb things create a domino effect of bad events.

I was no exception to these rules. While still hearing one of the twins getting their back readjusted by Gus, I started to make my way down to the bedroom with the open door. On my way, however, I got preoccupied for a second.

I noticed some car keys staring at me on the coffee table. Curious to know what kind of car these girls drove; I picked them up. Realizing they were keys to a Honda, I also observed something else on the key ring that sparked my interest. There was a black pouch about the size of a highlighter attached to the key ring. More

curious than ever, I opened it to see what was inside. Pepper spray. I liken discharging pepper spray to someone who had just informed you that they had farted. You already knew it was going to stink, but you end up smelling the air anyway in order to confirm the fart.

I pushed down on the pepper spray every so lightly. I took a whiff of the air. Nothing. Thinking the product had expired or was defective; I pushed down a little harder. I took another whiff of the air. Again, I couldn't smell anything. Next, I pushed down on the pepper spray like it was a bathroom air freshener and I was a houseguest who had just laid a stinky deuce.

This time I took a long deep whiff and opened up my nostrils like a sinus commercial, attempting to grasp every molecule of the spray that was within the air. I let out a cough so strong my eyes began to vibrate. I began hacking like a Mexican in a pick-up basketball game. As I continued to cough, I ran to the kitchen looking for water. I didn't even bother looking for a glass and ran straight to the kitchen faucet. I started gulping down the tap water like a dehydrated marathon runner.

One of the twins must have thought I was smoking some Acapulco Gold, because she came sprinting out of her bedroom.

TWIN: "Are you OK?"
ME: "Yeah, just got something caught in my throat. Which twin are you?"
TWIN: "Ava…"

Ava began to cough as well.

AVA: "What is that smell?"

ME: "I accidentally sprayed some of that pepper spray on the coffee table."

AVA: "What the hell did you do that for?"

I had no answer for my idiotic gesture but I, at least, was finally able to calm down and stop coughing. Ava started laughing at my pain.

AVA: "Aww…poor baby. Do you need me to take care of you?"

I nodded yes and played along with the game of doctor she was trying to initiate.

AVA: "Very well, let's step in the back to my office."

As we made our way to her bedroom, all I could think about was trying to take advantage of the moment.

AVA: "Lie down on the bed, and let me check your vitals."

I followed her directions and she put both of her hands up my shirt and started feeling all over my chest.

AVA: "Your heart rate seems a little rapid and the body heat you are emitting seems a little excessive. Let me check your stomach to make sure nothing is abdominal."

ME: "Abdominal? You mean abnormal?"

AVA: "Yeah, that too. You know what I mean."

Ava moved her hands down to my stomach and started feeling around.

> **AVA:** "Something doesn't seem right. Looks like I am going to have to do a full physical."

Unexpectedly, she went in for Wes Jr. Ava put her hands down my pants felt around and then clutched my balls.

> **AVA:** "Can you please turn your head and cough for me?"

Trying to keep myself from laughing, I continued to play along with the game and let out a slight cough.

> **ME:** "Is everything feeling normal down there, Doc?"
> **AVA:** "Not really, I am feeling some excess growth down here. Looks like I'm gonna need to check your throat."

Ava climbed on top of me and started kissing me. Next she went outside the scope of the game and got to the point.

> **AVA:** "Look. You and I both know why you are back here so let's just get this fuck out of the way."
> **ME:** "Let's do it Doc."

I couldn't wait to hear her yodel like a Swiss singer. We went from being fully clothed to being in our nature suits in a matter of seconds. It was time to get this show on the road.

We approached our sex session like two magicians with a few tricks up our sleeves. My first trick was putting my birdie inside her cage. I took my middle finger and put it in between her legs. Once he was inside, I moved him back and forth like a mime would.

AVA: "Mmm, your hands are so magical."

She started moaning with excitement. After a few birdie strokes, her mood suddenly changed.

AVA: "Ouch!"
ME: "Ouch? Wow, girl, you must be really tight."
AVA: "No it's not that...Wait...Stop. This is starting to hurt."
ME: "Am I doing it wrong?"
AVA: "No you are doing it right; it just started to really sting. Matter of fact, it stings really badly. I don't know what's wrong with me. This has never happened to me. What the fuck? I recently got tested so I know I'm clean."

I started feeling guilty because there was no doubt in my mind what was causing her vajayjay to sting. Ava was feeling the wrath of the pepper spray on my hands. However, she was still ready to move on to the next magic trick.

AVA: "It's my turn."

Ava settled on a card trick. She reached for my deck and grabbed my Ace of Spades. She got down on her knees and started sucking

my Ace. Ava was making my Ace disappear in and out of her mouth while simultaneously gripping it. Her other hand was preoccupied fondling my jokers. Before I was about to abracadabra-ala-kazam in her mouth I stopped her.

AVA: "Why did you stop me? Your dick is so delicious."
ME: "There are other things I want to do to you."

In actuality, I felt bad for lighting her poor little puss on fire because of the pepper spray residue on my hands. I was ready to break out my next magic trick to show her how sorry I was for burning her Puss In Boots.

I picked her up and laid her on the bed. She must have been anticipating my magic stick because her legs did like a couple on bad terms and parted ways. To begin my magic trick, I went down-town to taste her Queen of Diamond. I was able to make contact like Bausch & Lomb. I started to get into it as if I was eating a Sloppy Joe. This caused her to start directing my every action as if she was George Lucas.

AVA: "Yeah, keep eating my pussy."

This gave me more and more motivation to put in work like a 9 to 5. My tongue started doing the electric slide on her clit. Three licks to the left, three licks back, a muff dive forward, and 2 licks down, only to start it all over again.

Her left leg started moving like a Shake Weight. I knew she was on the verge of a climatic seizure. Then out of nowhere my mouth went numb. My lips started tingling. It was as if someone

was turning up the thermostat on my lips. My nostrils started flaring and my upper lip felt as if it was on the receiving end of a bad wax job. The stinging got so bad that my lips felt like a million red ants were biting them. My chin felt like I had an extreme case of razor burn.

I used the nearby bed sheet and tried to calmly wipe my face. Like a true professional, I maintained my cool and continued the job at hand. Less than a few seconds later, my cheeks felt as if they were being pricked by an intoxicated acupuncturist and my throat felt like I had eaten a habanero pepper from hell.

I stopped my electric slide, and quickly put my priorities in order. I began frantically fanning my hand in front of my face in an attempt to cool it down.

AVA: "Why did you stop? What's wrong?"

I barely managed to get out a word that could describe my current state.

ME: "Fire!"

Ava misinterpreted my word. Similar to most girl/guy interactions, there was clearly a lapse in our communication.

AVA: "Fire? You smell fire? Damn it! I forgot the brownies in the oven!"
AVA SPRUNG UP OUT OF THE BED, WHILE STILL IN HER BIRTHDAY SUIT.
ME: "No, wait."

She was already out of the bedroom before I could explain. The bedroom door had swung open making a loud thud noise in a desperate attempt to save the brownies. I heard Ava let out a big scream once she reached the end of the hall, as if there was a robber in the apartment. Then, I heard another scream followed by another scream.

Apparently, a naked Ava had startled both Addison and Gus, who were cuddled up on the living room couch. This created a scream fest between the three. Ava assumed that Addison was still getting her back blown out by Gus but she couldn't have been more wrong. An embarrassed, Ava quickly made her way back to the bedroom and slammed the door shut.

AVA: "Shit! Your friend just saw me naked!"

I was still in a state of panic and disregarded her statement. I was still fanning my face as if my name was Dakota. The flesh on my face felt like it was melting. Fearing my face was going to start looking like Freddy Krueger's in a matter of seconds, I began my search for water.

ME: "Where is the nearest bathroom?"
AVA: "First door on the left."
ME: "My face is on fire!"

As I made my way down the hall while cupping my face, I was incidentally bumping picture frames off the wall. Once I made it to the bathroom sink, I continuously splashed water over my face as if I was in a Neutrogena commercial. It only made the burning worse. Next, I turned the shower on and stuck my head under the showerhead in

attempt to ease the burning. It wasn't working! Water was all over the bathroom floor. In the midst of my chaos, I slipped and fell on the bathroom floor. I was now rolling back and forth while cupping my face.

All the commotion I was making caused everyone else in the apartment to direct their attention towards the bathroom. They were all now standing in the doorway looking at me as I tried to fight the invisible fire on my face.

ADDISON: "Is everything alright in here?"

I responded like an excited pyromaniac.

ME: "It burns, it fucking burns!"
GUS: "What burns? You got a STD that fast from her?"
AVA: "Fuck you, Gus!"
ME: "My face and my mouth, it's getting worse."
GUS: "What does it feel like?"

I gave Gus a sound bite that could have been straight from Beavis and Butthead.

ME: "Fire! Fire! Fire!"

Since Addison had already taken Chemistry 101 at Chico State, she thought she had all the answers.

ADDISON: "We need to counteract the chemical burning. It's like a jellyfish sting. Someone is going to have to pee on it."

GUS: "As in pee in his mouth?"

Ava co-signed her sister's prognosis. They had no idea what they were talking about.

AVA: "You are so smart, sis! I remember that from Chem Lab. The pH balance level in the pee helps to counter the acid venom in the stinging...or is it the other way around?"
ME: "What are ya'll talking about?"

Everyone ignored my inquiry because they were too busy debating amongst themselves. They continued to search for solutions.

ADDISON: "Ava, you're gonna have to pee on him. It's either got to be you or Gus."

Even Gus fell victim to their ignorant bullshit.

GUS: "I'll step up to the plate."

Gus stood over me and started to unzip his pants. I quickly rolled out of the way.

ME: "Nobody...AND I MEAN NOBODY is pissing on my face!"

A panicked Addison started to get more worried.

ADDISON: "Ava, call 9-1-1!"

AVA: "What's the number to 9-1-1? I mean do I have to dial a 1 first or can I just dial it?"

I quickly butted in.

ME: "Nobody is calling 911. I can muscle through this."

I was able to finally get myself off of the ground.

ME: "Everyone, out! I just need to try and jump in the shower."

With the water still running from the shower, Ava came and brought me a towel. After everyone left the bathroom, I was able to shower and clean myself up. This was the longest shower of my life. As streams of water from the showerhead hit my face, the burning on my face only intensified.

After about 30 minutes, the burning to my face eventually came to a halt. Finally, I had survived a pepper spray scare and made it out alive. I guess the saying is true, "Momma said that there would be days like this." Gus got to blow the back out of a twin and I almost became the man without a face. I typically enjoy pepper on most things that I eat, just not pussy. That weekend in Chico State with the twins helped to reinforce an important life lesson taught to me many years ago. **ALWAYS Wash your hands before you eat.**

Chapter 13

Fantasy Football

Tiffany was a diehard groupie sports fan and I had been blitzing her ass for a while. Everything in Tiffany's life revolved around sports. Tiffany and her girlfriends would have pop quizzes about who was on the current Dallas Cowboy's roster. One girl would blurt out a random number and Tiffany would promptly follow with a name. It didn't matter if a player was first string, backup or on the practice squad. These girls could rattle off every name on the team.

They even kept up with the latest trades and acquisitions by the Cowboys. What attracted me to Tiffany was that she was a semi-petite woman. This translated doing acrobatic tricks with her in the bedroom as if I was a part of the circus.

One evening during a Monday Night Football game, I was on top of Tiffany with my hockey stick in her goal. We were "pucking" with the lights off. The room wasn't completely dark, however, because the illumination from television provided us with just enough light to see each other's faces.

I picked Tiffany up like a plate of hot links at a black man's BBQ. With her legs wrapped around me, I put her against the wall. I started slamming her hole like a Michael Jordan highlight reel—I

was feeling like the greatest to ever play this game. I began putting in so much work; I started sweating like a hooker in church.

Suddenly, Tiffany started getting excited.

TIFFANY: "Oh...Yes, go baby!"

I started going faster.

TIFFANY: "Get it!"

My hip thrusts significantly increased in frequency.

TIFFANY: "Go, baby, go...yes....yes"

I went into supersonic speed and sped up as fast as my little hip flexors would allow. I was in Speedy Gonzalez mode. Tiffany screamed at the top of her lungs.

TIFFANY: "Woohoo!"

I released her from my grip. I was 99.9 percent certain that I had just given her the best orgasm of her life. Matter of fact, I would have put my whole life savings on it. In order to confirm, I double-checked with Tiffany.

ME: "Did you cum?"
TIFFANY: "Not yet silly. The Cowboys just scored!"

FML, my life savings and a 0.1 percent probability.

ME: "The Cowboys? How about we get back to me putting your back against the wall?"

Tiffany was till preoccupied by the television.

TIFFANY: "Hold on for a sec, they're about to kick the field goal."

This caused Tiffany to take a sip of who-the-phuck-are-you-talking-too. Not surprisingly, she immediately came to her senses. Soon after, we were able to finish what we had started.

While lying in bed Tiffany tried to have a heart to heart with me.

TIFFANY: "I think we need to change up our sex life."
ME: "Change it up?"
TIFFANY: "I mean I want more flavor, more spice. We always do it in the house. Don't you have any fantasies?"
ME: "Yeah, I fantasize about-"
TIFFANY: "...I want to do it on the football field. That's my fantasy."
ME: "The football field?"
TIFFANY: "Not just any football field. I want to do it in a stadium...on the fifty yard line."
ME: "Are you crazy? What stadium were you thinking? Let me guess Cowboy stadium."

Tiffany: "Not a bad choice. But I was thinking more on the safe side and going to my college stadium."

ME: "Yep, you're crazy."

TIFFANY: "Football is my favorite sport of all time. Since this is my fantasy, essentially we will be playing fantasy football. We can do it outside just like the actual players."

ME: "Why can't you have an indoor sport as your favorite sport? That way we can do it inside."

TIFFANY: "An indoor sport like what?"

ME: "Well, me personally, I love to motorboat. It's safe. You never hear about any injuries occurring when someone is motor boating. You can even do it the confines of your own home. How about we just motorboat instead of this fantasy football nonsense?"

Somehow, Tiffany convinced me to act out her fantasy.

Later that week, I drove over to the stadium to see what kind of security the stadium had. Since she went to a smaller school, security personal was minuscule.

Like a person planning a bank robbery, I scoped out the perimeter of the stadium and looked for every available entry and escape routes. Next, I brought my findings back to Tiffany's house and sounded like an army general prepping his soldiers for an ambush.

ME: "There is a gate on the south side of the stadium I think we can hop. Security is not the greatest because there is only one campus security patrol car that seems to come around every hour. I am not exactly sure how frequently security patrols at night. As long as we stay out of sight, we can get in there, do what we have to do and get out."

That night Tiffany and I set out on our excursion. Like thieves in the night, we dressed in all black and armed ourselves with flashlights. We pulled up to a semi-empty parking lot right outside of the stadium and walked towards the field bringing a blanket with us.

> **ME:** "I don't know if jumping the gate is such a great idea."
> **TIFFANY:** "You can't chicken out now. We're already here."
> **ME:** "Yeah, okay. Let's just get this over with."

I helped Tiffany climb over the fence and quickly followed. All of the stadiums lights were off. It was completely desolate with no sign of life. If it weren't for the bright moonlight shining above, it would have been impossible to see Tiffany. As we walked onto the field, we walked over the south end zone.

> **ME:** "OK, let's lay down the blanket right here."
> **TIFFANY:** "I want to lay it at midfield...on the fifty yard line. Isn't that what we agreed on? Why on earth would you want to do it in the end zone?"
> **ME:** "Because that way I can be scoring while I'm scoring."
> **TIFFANY:** "Come on! Grow some balls."

Reluctantly, I followed her to mid-field. Tiffany placed the blanket directly on the 50-yard line.

> **ME:** "You sure this is going to work? I mean what happens if we get caught?"
> **TIFFANY:** "It is a football stadium. Who is really going to catch us in here?"

ME: "Maybe...campus security or better yet the police."
TIFFANY: "Hurry up and give it to me, we are just wasting time arguing about this. Nobody is going to catch us. I think you are just being scared. The worst thing that will happen is that you might get a charge for trespassing."

At that point, it seemed as though Tiffany had bigger balls than I did. I went ahead and gave it a try. We only live once.

TIFFANY: "You seem very tense, let me help you relax."

Our fantasy football sex started out like we belonged to the AFC West in the NFL. She pulled out my man-in-motion and gave me some Arrowhead as if I was a *Kansas City Chief.* All of the Arrowhead made me want to do like *Oakland* and want to Raid-her. Next, I pulled her panties off and like *San Diego,* I *Charged* her. I started bucking her ass like a Denver Bronco. She went from being a tight end to a wide receiver, while I was making some forward progress. I stopped the play as if I heard a whistle.

ME: "You hear that?"
TIFFANY: "Hear what? Keep going!"
ME: "Shh…I hear something."
TIFFANY: "That's all in your head. I don't hear anything. You are paranoid for no reason."

I got back to my bump and run coverage under the moonlight. This time Tiffany stopped me shortly after I started back again.

TIFFANY: "I think I hear something now."

Like Phil Collins, *we could hear it in the air that night.* It just so happened to be the familiar sound of helicopter blades humming throughout the night air. We gazed up in the air looking to see where the sound was coming from.

ME: "Can you see anything?"
TIFFANY: "No."
ME: "Let's just wait for it to pass us."

The helicopter appeared suddenly above us as if it came through the line of scrimmage on an unsuspected blitz. The helicopter's spotlight was on. It was apparent that the police were looking for a suspect on the run.

ME: "Stay still. Just...don't...move."
TIFFANY: "He can't even see us. He is looking for a criminal anyway."
ME: "What do you think we are right now?"
TIFFANY: "Let's just keep going."

The helicopter pilot randomly directed his spotlight toward the field. While remaining undetected, the pilot moved the light around the football field in a circular motion.

Meanwhile, Tiffany's legs were high in the air as if they were trying to get a radio frequency from Saturn. She continued to gaze up at the helicopter.

TIFFANY: "You think he can see us from up there?"

In between all of the shucking and jiving I was doing in Tiffany's wide receiver, I managed to give her some reassurance.

ME: "There is no way he can see us. He would have directed the spotlight on us already."

However, it is hard to miss a naked man going third and long between a woman's goal posts even if it's from the air. Like a bowl of alphabet soup, I ate my words.

The spotlight moved directly toward us. Lights, camera, action! The spotlight was now on us as if we were stars in a Broadway play.

ME: "We might as well keep going. When you're in the spotlight you're supposed to shine."

Soon after making that statement to Tiffany, the Helicopter's spotlight turned off like electricity in the hood. Then back on, then off.

The spotlight flashed on and off five times. Each time the spotlight turned back on, it felt as if there was a sports photographer taking various action shots of me in an actual football game.

Flash one- Tiffany's legs were on my shoulders and her mouth was wide open as if she was yelling *audibles*.
Flash two- Tiffany's hands were wrapped around my back like she was making a tackle.
Flash three- My pelvis dropped back in anticipation that I would be hitting her down field receiver.

Flash four- My butt cheeks were squeezed together, my pelvis was forward. My man in motion was lined up all in her neutral zone.
Flash five- My footballs were getting spiked all over her backfield.

After the fifth flash, the helicopter continued flying over the stadium, looking for the suspect. My heart was beating faster than Pee Wee Herman in front of an adult theater.

> **ME:** "It's time to roll out of here before they dispatch someone."

Tiffany and I popped up and scrambled for our belongings as if there was a fumble on the field. I threw on my boxer briefs; Tiffany threw on her g-string. Next, I grabbed the rest of our clothes and we sprinted down the field toward the south end zone.

Since Tiffany was topless, her titties starting making a rhythmic clapping sound. They seemed to provide their own soundtrack for the moment. The sound caught my attention and I couldn't help but watch them like Rolex while we were running.

Once we made it back to the gate, we quickly climbed over it and put the rest of our clothes on. We scurried back to the car in the parking lot. Once we made it inside the car we sat there for a few minutes to catch our breath and make sure the coast was clear.

A few seconds later, we noticed a campus security patrol car pulling up to the stadium. We reclined our seats to avoid being detected. I peeked my head just over the car's window seal.

> **TIFFANY:** "What's he doing?"

ME: "He is out of his car and is walking around the perimeter of the stadium with his flashlight."

Soon as he was out of sight, I cranked up the car and we sped out of the stadium parking lot.

ME: "What an exciting night!"
TIFFANY: "We have to do this again sometime. I love this kind of fantasy football!"
ME: "Since you like it so much, then how about you lick on my *Buffalo Bill* the rest of the ride home?"
TIFFANY: "As long as you spike it in my mouth..."

Hip hip hooray to every football groupie like Tiffany and the men that can appreciate them.

Chapter 14

The Wingman Alliance

wingman has two definitions. A wingman may be referred to as a shooting guard or a forward in basketball who plays at the corners of the basketball court. A wingman may also be defined as a friend who assists another friend in getting a desired woman. One memorable night I was chosen to be the latter.

It was a Friday evening around 6pm and I was on the phone having a highly intellectual conversation with Andrea while watching a Padres game on TV.

ANDREA: "Are you even listening to me?"

ME: "Yeah, I'm listening."

ANDREA: "Answer my question."

ME: "I think so."

ANDREA: "You think so what? What did I just ask you?"

ME: "You asked me if your blow jobs are better with the Altoids or without the Altoids."

Andrea's voice was partially interrupted by Parker beeping in on the other line.

ANDREA: "So yes Altoid, or no Altoid?"
ME: "Yes, Altoid. Hold on this is Parker calling."
ANDREA: "No, I'm not going to hold 'cause I'm not done talking about this. This is really important to me."
ME: "Fine, I'll just call him back later."

My line beeps again. It's Parker once again.

ANDREA: "OK, I need to know what flavor you like."
ME: "Flavor? What do you mean? An Altoid is an Altoid; it only comes in one flavor...peppermint."
ANDREA: "That is not true, Mr. Wes. They come in cinnamon, ginger, peppermint, and spearmint..."

Parker rang in for the third time. My first instinct was that Parker's call was urgent, because he rarely called three times in a row.

ME: "Andrea, hold that thought. I have to go...let me call you back."
ANDREA: "Ugh, you always do that to me when it's something important!"

I quickly clicked over to see if Parker was alright.

ME: "Hey, what's up?"

I noticed Parker was driving in his car, and he sounded visibly upset.

PARKER: "Fuck that bitch!"

ME: "Isn't that what we are all trying to do?"
PARKER: "Fucking Carlee."
ME: "Slow down...What's going on?"
PARKER: "I just walked in her apartment and she was getting hammered by some dude that had a full sleeve of tatts."

Parker was a mess. He was in his first year of law school at the University of San Diego and had just witnessed his girlfriend of three years getting rocked by a Tommy Lee impersonator. Life sucks sometimes, and apparently so does Carlee. Parker just had to find out the hard way.

After Parker calmed down a bit, he asked me to come over. I turned off the game, jumped in the shower, and got ready to play psychologist. When I arrived at Parker's house, his face was beet red from all of the boozing he had done the past hour. He sat in his leather recliner sipping on a Miller Lite. He was like a bad pitch near home plate; down and out.

PARKER: "I can't believe this. Three years of my life and I have nothing to show for it. The guy was in there drilling her like he was looking for Saudi Arabian Oil."

I tried my best to lift Parker's spirits.

ME: "Well, look on the bright side, you're a free man, now.
PARKER: "I was faithful. Three years! Three fucking years!"

Parker in his drunken stupor all of a sudden gained super hero confidence.

PARKER: "Let's go out right now and crush some ass."
ME: "That's music to my ears."

Parker got up from his recliner, extended his arm out while holding the Miller Lite bottle and began to pour some beer onto the hardwood floor.

ME: "Parker? You alright man?"
PARKER: "Yeah, R.I.P to Carlee's puss. I witnessed it getting murdered today."
ME: "Snap out of it! Throw some clothes on, we are going out tonight."

Parker and I decided to try our luck at a place out in Del Mar, CA called Jimmy O's bar and grill. The bar was known for having rich Cougars that preyed on younger guys. The probability of Parker crushing lonely Cougar ass would be great. Even if we didn't end up with any women by the end of the night, at least Cougar hunting would take Parker's mind off of everything.

Before we got into the car to head over Parker stopped me in his driveway.

PARKER: "Hold on second. I'm only going to this place on one condition."
ME: "And what's that?"
PARKER: "You have to help me get ass. I need you to be my wingman tonight."

I put my hand over Parker's shoulder.

ME: "Of course! We're going to have a great time."

Parker quickly flung my hand away from him.

PARKER: "No...No...No. Look at me, in my eye."

Parker could barely stand straight on his own. I blew him off and started to walk to the car.

> **PARKER:** "Wait one minute. I'm not done. Are...you...going to be my wingman?"
>
> **ME:** "Yes, now get in the car."
>
> **PARKER:** "If you're going to be my wingman, then you have to take the wingman alliance."
>
> **ME:** "Will just put your drunken ass in the car so we can leave?"
>
> **PARKER:** "Nope. Not until you take the alliance. This is serious shit, dude."

Reminding myself that Parker had a rough day, I went along with his request.

> **PARKER:** "Put your right hand over your heart?"

I adjusted my posture so that I was upright and standing at attention. Enthusiastically, I placed my right hand across my heart like a second grader about to say the pledge of allegiance. Parker's equilibrium was off which made him swivel back and forth in one spot. It looked like he was playing with an invisible hula-hoop.

PARKER: "Are you looking at my eyeballs?"
ME: "Yeah, man! Come on its cold out here! You got me saying the pledge of allegiance in the middle of the neighborhood. Let's go--"
PARKER: "Shh...Shh..."

Parker tried to use some of his newly acquired law school voodoo jargon on me and tried to get technical.

PARKER: "It's not an allegiance, it's an alliance!"
ME: "Whatever it is, you need to pull yourself together...."
PARKER: "Just repeat after me! I'm cold, I'm bold and helping others get pussy, will never get old."
ME: "What in the-"
PARKER: "Say it dude."
ME: "I'm cold...I'm bold and...helping others get pussy, will never get old."

Parker was satisfied with me fulfilling his prerequisites for being his wingman. We had made it to the car and were finally on our expedition to partake in Parker's favorite pastime: Cougar Hunting.

During the entire drive to Jimmy O's I had to hear Parker complain about his current situation.

PARKER: "Un-fucking believable! I spend my Friday and Saturday nights in the law library studying Constitutional Law about how it's a woman's First Amendment right to have sex with whoever she wants and this bitch is putting it into practice!"

Parker continued his tirade and starting giving me personal details about his relationship with Carlee.

> **PARKER:** "She is the worst in bed! Half of the time I don't know if I'm fucking her or a corpse. She just lays there motionless. And her blowjobs...don't get me started. Speaking of the First Amendment, is it her First amendment right to give horrible blow jobs?"

I decided to answer Parker's rhetorical question.

> **ME:** "Technically, I think it might be her First Amendment right to give bad blow jobs. If she wants to express herself as an incompetent domoligist, she is well within her rights."
>
> **PARKER:** "Well she can take the Constitution and shove it up her ass...she likes everything else I shoved up there."

Parker continued with his rant. I heard about all the horrible things that Carlee did the previous three years from her atrocious cooking to the annoying giggling noises that she makes when she cums.

By the time we made it into Jimmy O's, Parker had somewhat sobered up, only to order more drinks. Often times when you are dealing with a drunk, time is never measured in minutes. Time is measured in drinks.

With that being said, approximately two shots and a half past a quarter beer later, we see a perfect 10 coming through the door. Not a ten as in a scale of one to ten. A ten as in there were two girls. One girl was an attractive skinny blonde, who was shaped

like the number one. She had legs so long, they made an ass out of themselves. Her friend on the other hand was a brunette and was shaped like the number zero. She was plump and juicy like a Thanksgiving turkey in The Hamptons.

Parker's attention immediately went to the skinny blonde.

PARKER: "You see the tall one over there?"
ME: "Yep, and I also see her hamburger shaped helper."
PARKER: "Smash or pass?"
ME: "Smash on the skinny one. Pass on the calorie collector."

Parker tried to put his law school jargon on me once again.

PARKER: "Remember, dude, you took the wingman alliance. If you violate its terms, you will have bad luck with pussy for the next seven years."
ME: "But she looks like the Michelin Man!"
PARKER: "Even the Michelin Man has needs..."

I remembered the wingman alliance, took a deep breath and reluctantly approached both women. I will never know why I always attract the "healthy" ones.

When I got over there, the fat girl was looking at me like a piece of meat. I wasn't sure if she wanted to put me in her fridge as a to-go plate or put me in her bed to get her in shape. Regardless, she was hungry for me.

I introduced myself in order to initiate first contact. The tall blonde told me that her name was Amanda and she was a model.

In the state of California when a girl tells you that she is a model, 90 percent of the time that translates to: "I'm unemployed." Everyone thinks they are a model. Unfortunately, reality is a dose often under prescribed. The bigger girl's name was Tish.

> TISH: "How is your night going so far?"
> ME: "It could be better. Do you ladies see that pathetic guy over there standing near the bar with his head hanging down?"
> AMANDA: "Yeah, he looks so sad."
> ME: "Well he caught his girl cheating on him a few months ago. She was the love of his life. He is very much heartbroken and he still hasn't gotten over it. I actually had to drag him out tonight. This is the first time that he has been able to go to a bar in months. He doesn't even remember how to pick up a woman because it's been so long. I think he is scarred for life."
> AMANDA: "Aww…I feel so bad for him. He *is* kinda cute! What girl would want to cheat on such a nice looking guy? Tell him to come join us."
> SYMPATHY: It's the one emotion that will cause a woman's legs to split in opposite directions.

I waived Parker over from afar to come join us. He and Amanda were hitting it off. Meanwhile, back at the fat farm, I kept Tish entertained. It wasn't too difficult because we just talked about our favorite foods and restaurants. Asking a plump girl about food was like asking the Kardashians what is was like to date a black man; it's what they do all day.

A quarter of a beer later, Amanda invited us over to her place. Everything was going as planned at the expense of my ego. Parker was getting closer and closer to crushing ass. On the other hand, I was so far below my expectatios that my pride was screaming, "code blue."

We took two cars on the way to Amanda's house. Parker rode in the car with Amanda and I sat in the other car with Tish. When we ended up at Amanda's apartment, thankfully she only had a one bedroom. This meant that I would not be getting seduced by the Tish.

Soon after entering the apartment and hanging out for a bit, Parker and Amanda headed for a private session in Amanda's bedroom. I was left on the couch with *Heavy T*.

After about five minutes of dead silence and twiddling our thumbs, Tish and I could hear moans and groans coming from the bedroom as if it was haunted.

TISH: "Wow, someone is having fun in there. Wish I could say the same thing for myself."

Did I just get called out by a 200 plus pounder? I couldn't risk the embarrassment of Parker walking in on me and giving Tish some of my frank and beans. However, Tish tried her best to corner me.

TISH: "So why are you holding back. You don't like big girls?"

ME: "It's not that I don't like big girls, I just have a lot on my mind. They say when you're stressed; the sex drive goes away."

Tish: "If stress is your issue then I'm sure I can alleviate that problem."

Me: "Thanks but I think I'll pass. I'm just going to chill tonight."

Tish decided to blackmail me into sleeping with her.

Tish: "Well, if you're not going to be doing anything then I'm going to knock on Amanda's door so you guys can leave."

I recited the wingman alliance in my head. *I'm cold, I'm bold and helping others get pussy will never get old.*

Me: "OK, whatever you do, don't knock on that door."

Tish: "You should just let me show you how a big girl does it."

Me: "School me, big girl."

Tish smiled and attacked my belt buckle. She then unzipped my pants. The Thanksgiving turkey was headed for my cucumber, *gobble gobble.* My fear of getting seduced by a fat girl had lapsed because the fear was no longer there. It was actually happening. I was now getting Domer Simpson on Amanda's couch.

She gave me head like an action movie; riveting, fast moving, violent, and thought provoking. I was about to jump out of my seat. I let out a big moan. Tish must have thought I was a doughnut because she sucked every bit of crème filling out of me.

Fifteen minutes after Tish sucked the life out of me, Parker walked out of the room and into the living room.

PARKER: "You ready to get out of here?"
ME: "Sure am."

Parker gave Amanda a hug; Tish gave me her number. I thought letting Tish give me head was enough giving for one night. By the time Parker and I reached the car, her number had already been deleted from my phone. My conscious had just suffered emotional shock. My pride was going to need some serious rehab and physical therapy.

When we got into the car, Parker was a new man.

> **PARKER:** "I could do this seven days a week! She was so
> hot! The mission was to crush ass, mission accomplished.
> Fuck Carlee! I just crushed Amanda's ass and I didn't have
> to hear an annoying giggle when she came."

Parker was so caught up in the excitement; he almost forgot to get a progress report and thank his wingman for "taking one for the team".

> **PARKER:** "How did it go with Tish? She seems like a really
> cool girl. You didn't try to bone her on the couch?"

I acted like I didn't hear him.

> **PARKER:** "You're not responding. OMG did you hook up
> with big Tish on the couch?"
> **ME:** "Let's just say I'm cold, I'm bold, and helping others get
> pussy just got old. This wingman now has limits."

Chapter 15

Out Of Time

Men are stubborn by nature and think that they can defy the laws of the universe. I am no exception. Although millions have tried and millions have failed, one thing remains constant on planet relationship.

Rule: Every player gets caught; it's only a matter of time.

In Asian philosophy, the *ying* and the *yang* are used to describe how polar opposites are interconnected in the natural world. Well in my world, I was dating two polar opposite females simultaneously, who were interconnected in the free world by my German army helmet. There was Angie and there was Gina.

Angie

Angie was the exact opposite of Gina. Angie was half white and half Filipino with the build of a European runway model. She was 6'1" and commanded a presence anytime she stepped into a room. Angie was what they called book smart.

She was a recent college grad from the University of Washington and graduated Magna Cum Laude. Not only was she a brainiac,

she loved to give brain. I initially got introduced to Angie randomly through one of my friends while taking Gina on a date to the movies.

Gina

I met Gina one night out in Seattle while playing pool at Belltown Billiards. Gina had to be one of the most attractive girls in the city. Unlike Angie, Gina had no formal education, yet she was street savvy. She was half German and half Mexican and would turn heads like Linda Blair in *The Exorcist*.

Her body frame was the yang to Angie's. She was 5'2" and had the perfect hourglass figure. Her measurements were literally 36,24,36. There was also a ten-year age gap between the two women. Gina was 32, and Angie was 22.

Gina had a feisty attitude but I had no problem putting up with it. She had a wet burrito stashed in her panties that was so good it would give a grown man temporary amnesia. During sex you would lose all cognitive ability. Just thinking about it makes me forget my name.

I had been exclusively dating Gina for a few months and then we started getting into petty arguments. We were both trying to be the Alpha male and in relationships, there can only be one alpha male.

She wanted to be in control of every aspect of the relationship and so did I. However, sex was our remedy for everything. We would fight then fornicate, fornicate and then fight. It got to a point where we were fighting while fornicating.

One morning, Gina is propped up on the kitchen counter while I'm eating her eggs and bacon. Then Gina taps me on the shoulder to ask me a question while my mouth was full.

GINA: "Excuse me, Papi?"

ME: "Yeah?"

GINA: "Do you think you'll take me to the mall after this?"

ME: "The mall? I'm trying to take you to ecstasy, and all you can think about is shopping?"

GINA: "Well, my legs are up in the air, and I happened to notice my feet. Since Nordstroms is having their huge sale right now, I thought you could take me to get something nice."

I got up from where I was eating her breakfast burrito.

ME: "How about this? I won't be taking you to ecstasy and I won't be taking you to the mall."

GINA: "Why do you have to be such an asshole all the time?"

ME: "Why do you have to act like a groupie all the time?"

GINA: "I can't help that I like the finer things in life."

I sighed and made a sarcastic comment under my breath.

ME: "Must be why you like this dick."

GINA: "I heard that!"

Like clockwork, our morning argument turned into sex on the counter. Gina and I had sex all the time. There remained one constant in our relationship; we had sex for every emotion. We had happy sex, angry sex, lazy sex, dirty sex, drunken sex. I know some other guy has been fucking you sex and the only reason I interact with you is because your gorgeous sex.

Then one day, the dynamics of our relationship changed. Gina started going off on me for no reason during a phone conversation.

ME: "I have been trying to call you for the past few days where have you been?
GINA: "I have been trying to grind and make money."
ME: "I can't get a call back, text, or some kind of smoke signal?"

Gina got defensive right away. At the time, I was still faithful to Gina. I was naïve to think that she didn't have some other guys on the side.

GINA: "You know what? I am sick of talking about this! Why don't you go and live your life because I am living mine. You are still young. Why don't you go out and date?"
ME: "Go out and date? What the fuck is that supposed to mean?"
GINA: "You're a smart guy you figure it out. I'm busy, and I have bills that I have to take care of."

Now, a woman giving me the green light to go out and date is like locking cookie monster up in a Nabisco plant and giving him an all you can eat pass. He may resist for a second then before you know it he is crushing every cookie in sight causing havoc. I became the cookie monster and started crushing every cookie I came in contact with.

In the midst of one of my cookie monster tirade, I was out at a charity event and came across Angie. Angie was with her girlfriends

and I noticed they were whispering and pointing in my direction. I zero in on Angie and approach her and her friends.

ANGIE: "Hey, Wes."
ME: "Oh, you remember me?"

Angie: "Yes, even though I met you briefly. Are you still with that one girl, I forget her name."

ME: "Gina."
ANGIE: "Yeah, Gina. That girl is beautiful."
ME: "It's complicated. I have not talked to her in weeks, and the last time I spoke with her she told me to go out and date because she is too busy for me."
ANGIE: "What a bitch! I would never tell you that if you were my man. You are too fine and sexy for that."

Needless to say, I continued to sit and talk with Angie for the rest of the night. We exchange numbers and started hanging out on a regular basis. One week went by, and I was already giving her my poon paddle.

Angie and I were inseparable. She was like one of the guys; she liked to play video games, loved to play basketball with me, and often times we would work out in the gym together. Anything I did, Angie was right there.

This went on for about two months and Gina was almost an afterthought. Almost. Then, one day I get a phone call from Gina while I was at Angie's place.

GINA: "Hey, Papi, I apologize that I have been MIA. I miss you so much and I love you. Can you come over tonight? I am making steak and enchiladas."

I hesitated for a moment, and then I thought about that wet burrito. The thought of that wet burrito made me lose all sense of reality.

ME: "Umm. Sure."

If food is key to a man's heart, then a wet burrito is the key to a man's brain, which is why men make stupid decisions when the sex is good. I was about to get both. The wet burrito will make a man drop everything he is doing, even if it is another woman.

As anticipated, when I arrived at Gina's house she feeds me, fucks me, and then cries on my shoulder, apologizing for the way she had been treating me.

The next night, Angie calls wanting to hangout. Being the generous person that I am, I accept the invite. Angie tried to top what Gina had done. Angie feeds me, fucks me and gives me a full body massage. Gina and Angie's pussies were like an ATM, I would deposit my baby gravy maker and instantly I would get results in the form of either money or benefits.

I could get use to this. All I had to do was show up and both women were treating me like a king. It was if one was trying to outdo the other. Gina was trying her best to get me back and Angie was trying to keep me.

Then, one night, things got heated between Gina and me after an acrobatic sex session. Gina had problems containing her feisty attitude. I finally got fed up with hearing her mouth so I left her

place in the middle of the night. When I reached the car, I dialed up Angie.

Angie answered on the first ring.

ANGIE: "Hey, babe, I was just about to call you and tell you goodnight. What are you doing up?"
ME: "I am leaving a friend's house, on my way home."
ANGIE: "Why don't you stop by? It's cold in this bed without you."
ME: "I'll be over there in thirty minutes."

Women have a sixth sense when it comes to other women so as soon as I walked through the door; I jumped in Angie's shower. Soon after that, I ate, climbed in bed, and Angie put my rhythm stick in her dick dungeon. This same routine happened for weeks. It was like clockwork.

I would have sex with Gina, and then we would get into an argument around 11:00 pm. I would leave Gina's and drive over to the other side of town to Angie's house. When I walked in the door, I would shower, eat and smash. It became like a dance routine. Fuck, fight, drive, shower, eat, fuck, and sleep. I was having sex with Gina then Angie. Angie then Gina, back to Angie.

I was having fun with both Gina and Angie until a man's worse holiday rolled around. Valentines Day. For guys, Valentine's Day is the equivalent to making an emergency tampon run for a woman at the grocery store. No guy wants to go through it but women need it.

I went back and forth in my mind as to what girl Iam going to spend Valentine's Day with. I could spend it with Angie but then

again I really like Gina. Angie was becoming my girl, and Gina was more of a slam piece.

It was a tough decision, so like masturbation, I decided to spend it by myself. That way if Gina or Angie wanted to talk with me on the phone, I could do so without having the other girl around.

I flew to LA for the week, happy that I could be by myself. However, my worst nightmare came true. Both of them insisted on being with me. My plan had completely backfired. I was left with no options than to spend it with both.

Angie flew from Seattle to LA, took a week off of work and we stayed locked up in a hotel room from the sixth to the fourteenth, having sex like we were the last people on Earth. During that time, any opportunity that I had away from Angie was spent trying to make reservations for Gina to come see me.

When it was time for Angie to leave, I felt like I had done a million ab crunches within the week. It was now Valentine's Day and after spending seven days with me, it was time for Angie to fly back to Seattle. Her flight was leaving at 4:00 pm from LAX, back to Seattle.

Meanwhile, Gina was flying in on Valentine's Day arriving in San Diego at 6:00 pm. LA to San Diego is a two hour drive and as soon as I dropped off Angie at LAX, I was speeding down the 405 highway in order to pick up Gina. Gina was only visiting for two days. She came to visit from the fourteenth through the sixteenth.

When I picked up Gina, we drove back to LA. Since I had not checked out of my hotel room, I kept the same one. The whole time we stayed at the hotel, we had I miss you sex. Between Gina

and Angie, I had put so many miles on that hotel bed; I knew it needed a tune up. No bed should be put through that kind of abuse.

One Saturday, after playing basketball with Angie, I finally decided that I was going to drop Gina and focus entirely on Angie.
When Angie was not around, I called up Gina and let her know
that it was over between us.

The next morning, while waking up next to Angie, I began to
get ready for a birthday brunch for one of my friends. As I was
running out of the door, Angie yelled from across the room.

> **ANGIE:** "Do you think we can hangout later? Maybe
> watch a movie?"
> **ME:** "Yeah that's fine, I will be thinking about you every
> minute, can't wait to see you later."

An hour into the birthday brunch, I get a call from Gina.

> **GINA:** "Things kind of ended abruptly last night. I really
> miss our old relationship, but if that is not what you want I
> understand. I really want us to work out and I'm sorry for
> the way I had been treating you."
> **ME:** "It is a little late for all of that. I'm actually at a birth-
> day party and can't talk. I have to go."
> **GINA:** "All I'm asking for is fifteen minutes of
> your time. Can I come talk to you later? How
> does seven sound?"

I was determined to let Gina go and a fifteen-minute conversation
would not hurt.

ME: "Yeah, we can talk then. I will see you later."

As soon as I hung up the phone, I remembered my plans with Angie. So I immediately called Angie. The phone rang and I got a voicemail.

VOICEMAIL: "Hello, you have reached Angie, leave a message."

I gave a pathetic impersonation of someone who with the common cold.

ME: "Angie I am feeling really sick, and I am going to have to cancel our plans tonight. I'll give you a call tomorrow I hope that you had a good day."

Upon hanging up the phone, I rushed home in order to clean my place up before Gina got there. When Gina arrived, she looked amazing and all I could think about was wet burrito. She had a jogging suit on and a sports bra.

GINA: "Papi, do you have a minute? I was on my way to work out but just wanted to talk for a bit."
ME: "Yeah, I'm listening."
GINA: "The past few months, I have not been the best woman for you. I want to apologize for everything that I have put you through the past few weeks. I really miss you."

I could barely make out what she was saying. I completely zoned out. Her mouth was, moving but the only thing that I heard was "I have a wet burrito, I have a wet burrito, and I have a wet burrito."

GINA: "Well?"

I came back to reality.

ME: "Well, what?"
GINA: "I just asked you if you wanted to sit and watch a movie. That way we can cuddle."
ME: "Sure."

Ironically, I select the movie *Out of Time* starring Denzel Washington. Halfway through the movie, Gina starts massaging me, kissing on my neck and getting me all hot and bothered. I am unable to concentrate, and even though Denzel is talking, it is as though he talking directly to me. All I hear out of his mouth is, "Wes, she has a wet burrito."

All of this commotion in the room causes my sperminator to rise. So I decide to take a "commercial break" and pause the movie. Once the movie gets paused, Gina does an impersonation of a professional polo player; she grabs my mallet, goes for my balls and rides me. Twenty minutes and four sex positions later, I'm dripping with sweat as if I have just left the sauna. I am left there pondering why the wet burrito is so good to me.

Still drenched in sweat, I end the commercial break and un-pause the movie. The wet burrito must have had MSG in it because I began to get sleepy. We had just worked each other out like a 9 to 5.

I found myself about to doze off when Gina grabs my arm and gives me a look as if my place is haunted.

GINA: "Do you hear that?"

I'm in disbelief thinking that she is playing games with me.

> ME: "Hear what?"
> GINA: "I keep hearing a knocking"
> ME: "That's all in your mind. Sometimes, sex can be so good you start to hear things."
> GINA: "No, I'm serious...listen."

I listen intensely, I hear nothing.

> GINA: "Wait...turn the movie down."

I turn the movie down and listen patiently. Then I hear it clear as day.
KNOCK, KNOCK.
There is no denying that knock. I look at Gina.

> ME: "Who would be knocking at the door this late at night? It's eleven o' clock."
> GINA: "Go get the door or at least see who it is."

I was hoping that whoever this individual knocking at my door is not Angie. Not in a million years would it be Angie because she knows that I am sick and I told her that I couldn't hang out with wher tonight.

Next, I tiptoe as slow as I can to the door, hoping the person will just go away. As I arrive closer to the door I hear the knocking get louder. It has reached a banging level by now. I slowly look through the peephole and sure enough there she is. Angie. My heart started racing faster than a thoroughbred on speed in a Kentucky derby.

At this point, I had three choices:

Talk to her through the door and tell her to come back

   1. Open the door and talk to her outside my place and make
      sure she doesn't come in.
   2. Do the cowardly thing and act like nobody is home.

I played it safe and selected option three. I did an about face and
walked real slow back to my bedroom. Finally the knocking stopped.

   As I approach the bedroom, Gina is sitting there with her panties and bra on.

   GINA: "Who was that?"

I answer truthfully, yet sarcastically.

   ME: "It was just one of my girls."

Gina laughs it off and questions me again.

   GINA: "No really, who was at the door?"
   ME: "I told you, one of my girls."
   GINA: "Whatever, I'm about to answer the door and see
   who it is."

I call Gina's bluff.

   ME: "Go ahead."

At this point, I was hoping that Angie had left the building. However, I remember the law of planet relationship. "Every player gets caught; it's only a matter of time."

I didn't really think that she was going to get up and answer the door but she did. Gina walks towards the front door as I sit on my bed. Everything happened in slow motion. I could hear the front door open. I knew that Angie had left since all of the knocking had ceased.

My conclusion was suddenly disproven.

I heard Angie's voice.

ANGIE: "Hi, is Wes here?"

GINA: "Yeah he is here. Come on in? He is in the back bedroom."

ANGIE: "Thanks."

I could hear Angie's heals making contact with my hardwood floors as she made her way down to my bedroom. When Angie made it to my doorway, I was sitting at the edge of my bed in my boxers, with no shirt on.

ANGIE: "Wes, you wanna tell me what's going on here? Well, it's obvious 'cause you're still sweaty in your fucking boxers and she is in her lingerie. You must have just got done fucking, which explains why you couldn't answer your fucking door!"

Gina chimes in.

GINA: "I'm so confused. What's going on here? And who do you think you are talking to him like that?"

Angie looks Gina up and down.

ANGIE: "Are you and Wes still together?"

Gina remained confused.

GINA: "Uhhh, yes? Can I help you?"

Angie drops a potent bomb to enlighten the situation.

ANGIE: "Where have you been the last two months because he has been sleeping at my place every night?"

Gina laughs the embarrassing disclosure off.

GINA: "That's funny because he has been at my place the past two months so I know your lying."

Angie turns her attention towards me.

ANGIE: "What the fuck? So that explains why the first thing you do when you come to my place is take a shower in the middle of the night. It's because you have been fucking her!"

Gina finally realizes what has been going on for the past few months.

ANGIE: "I came over here because you said that you were sick and I was trying to make you feel better by bringing

you soup. Is there something that you want to say to the both of us?"

I remained calm, and with a straight face, looked at Angie remorsefully.

ME: "I am sorry for my actions; it was wrong of me."

However, in the back of my mind, I was saying, "If you had access to that wet burrito, like I did, you would have done the same."
Next, I look at Gina.

ME: "You told me to date other people and that is what I did."

Gina's face turned beet red.

GINA: "I said DATE other people, not go around fucking them right after you fuck me!"

Both women started tag teaming me with verbal obscenities. They sounded like music producers with various renditions and remixes of fuck you, you bastard, son of a bitch, you asshole and how could you do this to me.
Angie pulls me by the hand.

ANGIE: "Gina, do you think I can talk to Wes in private?"
GINA: "Be my guest. Do whatever you want with that bastard. I am done!"

As soon as I left the room with Angie, I could hear Gina in my bedroom throwing my furniture around from wall to wall like it was a sport.

Angie began to cry.

ME: "I know what this looks like, but I promise to clear everything up by morning."

ANGIE: "Do you even care about me? How could you do this to me?"

ME: "I will explain everything to you tomorrow, but right now you have to leave because it is about to get ugly in here."

Soon after saying said that, we heard Gina throw another piece of furniture.

ME: "See, Gina is the craziest woman I know. She has that Mexican side coming out of her. I'm fearful for my life right now. She will kill both of us, if you don't leave right now."

I had almost convinced Angie to leave when all of a sudden Gina comes in the living room and started speaking Spanish to me.

She started making demands in Spanish, then translated them to English.

GINA: "This bitch has to go, if you care anything about us. Make this bitch leave before I make her."

Gina heads to the kitchen and it appears she is going to grab a knife in order to make Jack-0-Laterns out of all of us.

I turned toward Angie.

ME: "Angie, you have to go...as in now!"

Angie apparently did not realize the severity of the situation. She was only thinking about her hurt feelings and had no idea Gina was about to carve a smile in her face like the Joker.

ANGIE: "Why do I have to go when I have been nothing but nice to you, and that bitch has caused you nothing but trouble?"

I whisper in Angie's ear.

ME: "I'm going to call you in twenty minutes, just leave for now because I am worried about our safety."

I was hoping Angie was going to follow my advice because she didn't know who she was messing with. There were things I knew about Gina that Angie had no idea about. For example a few people knew how psycho Gina could get when she was upset. For example, she once went after her ex-boyfriend with a shotgun when she caught him cheating on her. So fearing for our safety was a fair assessment of the situation.

Gina continued to search for knifes in the kitchen. However, as a safety precaution, I hid my kitchen knives prior to Gina's arrival that night.

ANGIE: "Fuck you, Wes! I fucking hate you! I hope you marry that tramp."

Angie stormed out of my place, slamming the door behind her. As soon as she left, Gina started crying.

> **GINA:** "You know what? This is my fault. We can get past this; just promise me that this is over. I don't want another bitch to come between us."

Gina started to cry hysterically. I began to hold her in my arms as tight as I could to let her know that everything was going to be all right in order to diffuse the tension in the room.

> **GINA:** "Promise me she won't come back in our lives."
> **ME:** "I prom…"

Before I can even make the promise, Angie storms back into my place. I had failed to lock the door behind her when she left. At the top of her lungs, Angie yells.

> **ANGIE:** "I don't understand why I have to leave? Why can't she leave? After all I'm the one that has been there for you. All she ever did was use you."

During that situation, I had to think fast, and so I came up with a lame excuse.

> **ME:** "Angie, I did invite Gina over."
> **ANGIE:** "So what the fuck does that mean?"
> **ME:** "Well you came over unannounced and uninvited, so you have to leave."

ANGIE: "You know what Wes? I said it before, and I am going to say it again. Fuck you!"

While looking at Gina to make sure she was not going to do anything crazy, Angie blind sides me with an open hand smack to the face.

ANGIE: "Asshole."

When Gina witnesses this she charged Angie and starts swinging.

GINA: "I got your asshole right here, bitch."

As Gina swung, she barely missed Angie. I then tried my best to hold Gina back from annihilating Angie.

ME: "Angie, it's starting to get ugly; you have to leave or else I'm calling the cops."

The threat works and Angie stormed out of my place once again. I run to the door and immediately locked my front door.

I calmed Gina down once more.

GINA: "Can you take me back to my place so that I can get some fresh air? This is just too much for me! I don't want that crazy bitch breaking in your place again."
ME: "Good idea; let's get out of here."

I walked towards my car and only to find that Angie had decorated my car with red lipstick. The artwork consisted of catch phrases such

as "you're a cheater, you fucked with the wrong girl, and kiss my ass". Gina and I had some time cleaned my car off as best as we could.

GINA: "I'm ready to go home now."

I dropped off Gina and went back home.

It was the first time I had slept in my bed for months and it felt good. I was not thinking about Angie nor Gina's wet burrito.

That night I came to the realization that my ying and yang relationship was out of time like the movie I had never finished. I learned that it is very hard to have your cake and eat it too. Lastly, I contemplated the law on planet relationship, which came true in the end: **Every player gets caught**.

What I failed to mention, was that getting caught is not always the worst thing that can happen to a player. Within two weeks of this story, I was once again smashing both Gina and Angie.

Out of time? Apparently, I got a time extension.

Chapter 16

College State Of Mind

The things that I love about a big college campus atmosphere are the school spirit, the nice facilities, and most of all: the college state of mind. The college state of mind means different things to different people. For me, the college state of mind was a time when you lived carefree. It was the first time living away from home with thousands of other kids that were just as ignorant about real life as you were.

It was a time where all you thought about was the location of the next big party, having one-night stands on top of nightstands, and figuring out the cheapest methods to replenish your condom supply.

This was the college state of mind. Alexis was the girl that brought me back to memory lane while visiting Penn State University in State College, Pennsylvania.

If you have never been to Penn State's campus, go. And if you have been there then I don't need to tell you to go again. Penn State is a gem in of itself. After a cold winter, spring brings with it, beautiful trees, friendly people and parties happening every second.

There are vertical smiles everywhere. Combine that with a DUI rate that is higher than Snoop Dogg on an Amsterdam vacation and you have a fornication frenzy. Sex is not only in the air;

it's in the alley, in the back of the club, in the public restrooms and the back of a few SUVs. During my brief time in State College, sex also happened to be in my hotel room.

My First Day

I had heard all of the stories about how great this small college town was. Eager to see what State College had to offer, I headed out in pursuit of a college state of mind.

Walking down the main strip of College Avenue, the first thing I noticed was all the women's outfits. These outfits were walking billboards advertising nothing but assets. It was like walking through the red light district with a million dollar gift card. It was all-free.

I ended up at a bar called The Lion's Den. There was no cover and the place often attracted college students because the liquor was inexpensive. Cheap liquor and no cover situated in a decent atmosphere often equates to drunken college students making a bunch of bad decisions.

While at the Lion's Den, I began watching the front door to see what types of vertical smiles were coming through the doorway. Not even in Vegas could I have had better odds. It seemed as though the door was randomly generating hot girl after hot girl. It was going to be like fishing with dynamite.

Most of the women that were prancing through the door were drunken blondes. I'm not saying there is anything wrong with a drunken blonde, but I was looking for more of a challenge.

Bagging a drunken blonde in a state college is like receiving a fortune cookie from the local Chinese restaurant. You never ask for it but they are determined to give it you anyway.

After watching blonde after blonde walk through the door, I couldn't help but notice the tall Brazilian when she walked through the door. She stood out like a cold pair of nipples. Bingo! *Something exotic to quench my thirst.*

Enter, Alexis. Her legs were so long they definitely made an ass out of themselves. She was extremely tall with an athletic build. So like an athlete, I let the games begin.

I walked over toward Alexis and introduced myself.

ME: "I noticed you as you walked in. I'm Wes."

We shook hands and she seemed somewhat intrigued by my presence.

ALEXIS: "I don't recognize you. Are you new to this area?"

I stuck out my chest and lowered my voice one decimal level in order to exert my manhood.

ME: "Yeah, I am one of the new Penn State recruits."
ALEXIS: "Oh, really? What sport?"

I quickly thought of a sport known for having generous groupies and bountiful baby mothers.

ME: "Football."

Alexis rolled her eyes in disgust.

Alexis: "Doesn't surprise me. You football players are all the same. You think you can get any girl you want and you feel that the

world owes you something. I hope you don't get big headed like the rest of those football players."

ME: "Hey, I'm just the new recruit. Give me a break."

ALEXIS: "Yeah but you're still a football player. They're all the same. I don't deal with 'em."

That is the risk you take when tell a girl something you're not. Her attitude towards me completely changed. I was trying to impress and she could care less. The more I tried to talk to her, the more she blew me off. The dynamics between us had instantly changed. It must have been my lucky day, however, because her attitude quickly did a 180 toward the positive. As she looked up, her face turned white like she had seen a ghost. She quickly grabbed my hand and pulled me to the bar and started leading me to the opposite side of the establishment.

ALEXIS: "Come on, let's go have some drinks."

We made it to the bar, the bartender knew her by name, and she ordered three tequila shots all for herself.

ALEXIS: "Sorry, did you want one?"

ME: "No...I'm okay. But thanks."

Alexis wrapped her arm around my waist. Then leaned over and whispered in my ear.

ALEXIS: "Do me a favor."

ME: "Yeah."

ALEXIS: "Don't leave my side and act like we're together."

ME: "Are you alright? Two seconds ago you were saying that you weren't interested. Now you're acting like we are married. You ever heard of taking it slow?"

Alexis was a nervous wreck.

ALEXIS: "My ex-fiancé is here."

ME: "Ex-fiancé?"

ALEXIS: "Yes, and I really don't feel like seeing my ex. Let's get out of here. Can we just leave this place already? I think I need a cigarette."

Alexis downed her last shot. Next she squeezed my hand tightly and maneuvered her way through the crowd like a celebrity in the midst of a sea full of paparazzi. Once we got out of the club she somewhat calmed down.

ALEXIS: "Do you have a car?"

ME: "Yeah, I have this rental the football team gave me."

ALEXIS: "Wait…isn't that a NCAA violation? Never mind. That's not important now. The football team is always doing shady shit."

Next, Alexis got in the passenger seat of my car.

ME: "OK, so where are we headed? Your place or mine?"

ALEXIS: "Mine."

While in the car riding to her place, my mind began to wonder. I was already thinking about my game plan and how I was going to get her in the sack. Then she shook my shoulder while I was in mid thought.

ALEXIS: "…Hello? Are you even listening to me?"
ME: "What did you say?"
ALEXIS: "I said make a right at this next street. You are about to pass my place."

Finally we reached her place. I parked, turned the car off, and unbuckled my seat belt. I was already planning on hitting her with my mule once we got into her bedroom. Then she played me like bench warmer. She refused to let me in the game.

ALEXIS: "I really enjoyed hanging out with you tonight. Thank you for the ride. I am going to head to bed, take care."

I stood there dumbfounded as she reached over to give me a hug and a kiss on the cheek. Before I could gather my thoughts and respond, she quickly made it out of my car and sprinted to her front door. She yelled from her doorstop as she opened her front door.

ALEXIS: "I will text you tomorrow. Have nice night."

The only thing that was getting turned on that night was my car engine so that I could make my way back to the lonely hotel room. So much for going with something *exotic*. I was unable to seal the deal with Alexis.

My Second Day

My first day in State College was a huge disappointment. I passed on all the easy sleazy blondes, only to get denied by the exotic Brazilian. I was determined that, on my second day at State College, I would get one of these hot blondes to put me in a college state of mind.

Admittedly, I was skeptical that I would ever hear from Alexis again. Much to my dismay, Alexis sends me a text message. It read: "Sorry about last night, I just got a little emotional when I saw my ex. Do you want to hang out at my place and pre-game for tonight? I promise you won't be disappointed."

Here we go again. Alexis was just another woman out there to play games with me. She clearly had feelings for her ex-finance. With so much ass to crush and another 18 year-old hottie being produced every second throughout the world, who wants to be bothered with games?

Since it was somewhat early in the day and I had nothing better to do, I reluctantly agreed to meet her at her place. When I arrived, she already had drinks made. It was clear to me that she had been sipping for some time. She was already a little tipsy and started to express her true feelings. I started asking her questions as if I was Piers Morgan.

ME: "So you were engaged. Tell me a little about that."
ALEXIS: "Yeah, I was then I got cheated on. It was the love of my life. That is really what brought me out here. Now, every time I see my ex, the feelings start to come back."
ME: "So is that why you don't care for football players?"

ALEXIS: "No, they just always tried to hit on me even though they saw that I had a huge ring on my finger. It also didn't help that I found out my ex was sleeping with a guy on the football team."

I almost fell out of my chair.

ME: "He was gay? You mean to tell me that your ex was getting his Jerry Sandusky on?"

Alexis just shook her head.

ALEXIS: "I don't know what my ex was doing out there. She would lie to me about everything. Lies, lies, and more lies. Finally, I couldn't take it anymore."

I was confused. Her story was not making sense to me and my comprehension ability seemed to be at first grade redneck level.

ME: "I...I'm so confused. I heard you say she. Who is she?"
ALEXIS: "My ex."

I paused for ten seconds and replayed everything this girl had just explained to me for the past few minutes. Alexis saw the confusion on my face and gave me an alley op towards my moment of clarity.

ALEXIS: "If you have not figured it out yet, I play for both teams."
ME: "So you were engaged to a..."

ALEXIS: "Yep. A woman. When I say I play for both teams, I'm not talking no *junior varsity*. I'm talking *varsity*."
ME: "Varsity?"
ALEXIS: "Yeah, as in, I'm no amateur, I do both and I'm great at both. I can run with the big dogs. I'm a pro at what I do."

Alexis had now put me in a college state of mind. Not only was opportunity knocking at my door, it brought with it an RSVP invitation to threesome avenue. She had me smiling like a butcher's dog.

ME: "So when do I get to try out for the varsity team?"
ALEXIS: "Patience, my friend. Even Michael Jordan didn't play on Varsity right away."

As the night matured, we stepped out to *Infernos*, a local bar. I noticed that she was checking out women like I was checking out women.   It became obvious that she had an infatuation for roast beef curtains.

It was evident that she was bisexual. She loved women just as much as she loved men. Once the bar started to become crowded, we began to people watch. It was like hanging out with one of the guys.

ME: "What do you think about her?"

I pointed to the attractive brunette that had just walked past us.

ALEXIS: "She is okay. Cute face. No body."

ME: "Really? I thought her body was pretty good."
ALEXIS: "It is just average. Don't get me wrong, I'd still hit it."

I nodded my head in agreement.

ME: "I would definitely hit it."

Alexis pounced on the potential opportunity.

ALEXIS: "Well, quit being a bitch, and let's invite her over tonight."

Before I could respond to her, Alexis was already in hot pursuit. She walked over and, with her hand, caressed the girl from her shoulder down to her wrist.

ALEXIS: "Your dress is almost as hot as you are!"
GIRL: "Why, thank you!"

The girl lustfully looked back at Alexis with an "I will eat your *cho-cha* all night long if you let me" type of look. They were trading infrared gaydar signals back and forth to each other.

GIRL: "You're hot as well! I love those red pumps you're wearing."

It was if they knew that one another's favorite sport was muff diving. They were telepathic clit lickers. Then the girl noticed me standing right there and turned her attention over to me.

GIRL: "OMG, is this your girlfriend?"
ME: "Umm-she-is- just-"
GIRL: "Well, she is smoking! And so are you! The things I would do to the both you..."

I couldn't believe my ears. My ears even couldn't even believe my ears. My bisexual just picked up another bisexual right in front of me. I was in more disbelief than an Atheist at Sunday school.

Alexis grabbed her hand and positioned herself closer to the girl.

ALEXIS: "Where are you going after this?"

Before the girl could answer, her drunken boyfriend swooped in out of nowhere and goal tended the potential threesome. He came in stumbling and mumbling.

BOYFRIEND: "Come on, babe. Let's go, remember we were supposed to catch up with Jason and the rest of the crew."

Obviously disappointed, the girl apologized on behalf of her cock-blocking boyfriend.

GIRL: "Sorry, you two. He is really drunk and I need to take care of him."

Her boyfriend lost his grip on the beer he was holding and it shattered on the floor. His girlfriend became embarrassed for her man and picked up the large pieces of glass from the floor.

The situation reminded me of Bill Clinton getting some Lewinski. He came fast and even though he made a fool of himself, she was right there to swallow his pride.

My fantasy started to fade like a black t-shirt from Wal-Mart. Two pairs of titties had just dwindled down to one. Alexis and I stayed at Infernos a little while longer then we ended up where most tramps feel right at home; my hotel room.

Things happened really fast once we arrived in the room. Before we knew it, both of us had our varsity uniforms on. She was wearing nothing but a necklace. I was wearing a pair of socks on my feet and a condom on my meat.

She turned around and did her best impersonation of a compass. She put her ass in the air so it faced north. She put her head down on the pillow so that it faced south. She reached behind her and grabbed my hips. One of her hands reached around from the east, and the other hand came in from the west and she pulled me in close.

Once I entered the Republic of Labia, she gave me my working visa.

ALEXIS: "I want you to give it to me rough."

I began to wage war on her cervix. I went in for the kill.

Apparently it wasn't enough. It was like bringing a knife to a gunfight. She started backing her ass back up on me like a dump truck. I held on for dear life. I was clearly outmatched. Her vajay-jay was the elementary school bully that was taking my lunch money. I had nowhere to go.

Like a bully, her demands became louder and with more frequency. My pecker was getting taken to lunch.

ALEXIS: "Harder, Harder, Harder. Smack that ass."

I smacked her right butt cheek so hard that it sounded like a rim shot from a snare drum. It echoed throughout the room. It didn't even faze her.

ALEXIS: "Come on, hit me harder! I told you I played
varsity didn't I? Didn't I tell you I played varsity?"

I...could...not...even...answer...her...question. My mouth was moving but even my words were in the midst of operation retreat. My words were scared to come out of my mouth. Her bald biscuit was annihilating my pecker. It was chewing him up only to spit him back out. She was kicking ass and taking names.

Like a wimpy kid who finally decides to stand up to the playground bully, my pecker and I fought back. I began to give her left gluteus maximus a few combinations; Judo style. Left hand slap, right hand slap, pelvic thrust. Overhand slap, pelvic thrust, pelvic thrust, double hand slap, right hand uppercut, pelvic thrust, cross hand right slap, left hand double slap.

ALEXIS: "Yes! Yes! Yes!"

I was finally gaining some of my leverage back. I started scolding her cucumber canal like a problem child.

ME: "Don't!"

Pelvic thrust.

ME: "You."

Double pelvic thrust.

ME: "Ever!"

Three quarters thrust.

ME: "Question."

Pelvic Thrust.

ME: "My."

Triple pelvic thrust

ME: "Varsity."

Pelvic thrust.

ME: "Skills."

I was finally standing up to the bald biscuit bully. I went into beast mode. I gave Alexis everything I had. I gave her the works. My hips were going every which way like a malfunctioned Carousel. I was doing the wobble while in her kitty cage.

ALEXIS: "What the fuck is happening to me?"
ME: "What do you mean?"

Alexis repeated herself a few times.

> **ALEXIS:** "This has never happened to me."
> **ME:** "What has never happened to you?"
> **ALEXIS:** "I'm going to cry. I am *really* going to cry...Oh wait, I'm going to cum. I don't know whether to cum or cry."
> **ME:** "Did you say cum or cry?"
> **ALEXIS:** "Yes, but keep going it feels so good. Oh shit, I'm going to cry."

I was at a loss for words and short on advice.

> **ME:** "Do both of 'em."
> **ALEXIS:** "Oh fuck, I'm crying, I'm crying. I can't believe I'm crying."

Alexis turned and looked over her shoulder to where I was. Sure enough there were tears trickling down her cheek. She started laughing.

> **ALEXIS:** "Why am I crying right now? OK, stop. I need a moment."

I anchored my boat and stopped swimming in her ocean. Alexis put her face in the pillow in order to wipe the tears off of her face. She took a brief twenty-second time out.

> **ALEXIS:** "What the fuck was that? That has never happened to me. You were fucking me so good; I was actually crying."

Then, she went carried on like nobody's business.

ALEXIS: "Oh well, let's proceed."

I began where I left off. I got angry at her coochie. I started again with my Judo style combinations. Left hand slap, over hand slap, pelvic thrust. Shortly thereafter, Alexis tried to broadcast her current actions throughout my hotel. Her voice rang like the Liberty bell.

ALEXIS: "I'm cumming, I'm cumming! Ohhhhhh, you son of a bitch, I'm cumming!!!"

Her body shook violently as if she had gotten tased with 5,000 volts. She fell over on her side and continues to have convulsions. I had just slayed the dragon with my sword.

ME: "Hello? You still alive over there?"

My man pickle was still ready to rock and roll in case she got up again. I felt confident again and started talking trash to her.

ME: "My dick is like alcohol; you should only take it in moderation. Otherwise, you end up on the floor curled up in a ball."

She shot back with a hint of sarcasm.

ALEXIS: "Ha-Ha. Very funny."
ME: "Come 'on let's get back at it. I'm ready to keep going."

Alexis shook her head.

> **ALEXIS:** "I need a minute; actually, give me two. I am done."
> **ME:** "Done? What do you mean done? What about me?"
> **ALEXIS:** "What about you? You didn't cum?"
> **ME:** "No..."
> **ALEXIS:** "Sucks for you! Honestly, I came, and I can't go for a while...that was intense for me."

At that point, I felt left out in the cold.

> **ME:** "All that mess you were talking. I thought you played varsity? My magic flute needs to be played right about now."

It is amazing how competition brings out the best in us. Upon hearing those words, Alexis came back to life. She grabbed my pickle.

> **ALEXIS:** "Here, give me this thing."

She then made a mockery out of the 10,000-hour rule. The 10,000 hour rule as mentioned in the book *Outliers* by Malcolm Gladwell; states that the key to success in any field is being able to practice that specific task for a total of 10,000 hours. Once you have achieved 10,000 hours of practice during a lifetime in any particular area, then you have become an expert in that field.

By the way, Alexis was playing my magic flute, I never doubted that she had shattered the 10,000-hour rule. She may have even

doubled it. I would've been shocked if she didn't have 20,000 hours worth of practice playing magic flutes. She was an expert in the field. Alexis was like a soul train dancer, she didn't miss a beat.

After what seemed was 2.2 seconds, she made my weasel go pop. Not only did she make me cum, she made my cum, cum. If I were on the board of trustees at Penn State, I would have given her a full ride swallowship.

After my weasel popped she kept going. Her mouth was demanding more than what my little testes could produce. Alexis caused my sperm count to be placed on back order.

I pushed her head away.

ALEXIS: "Why are you pushing me away?"
ME: "There is nothing left! **Nothing.** All my reserves are gone."
ALEXIS: "Do you need me to keep going?"
ME: "NO! The well is dry. You got me all dehydrated. Matter of fact, you owe me some electrolytes."

Alexis laughed and then licked some of my steamy mayonnaise from her fingers.

ALEXIS: "Mmmm, your cum tastes delicious. It's really sweet. I can drink this all day."

Like a spoiled kid at Disneyland, Alexis was demanding another turn.

ALEXIS: "I want to do it again!"

ME: "You just got done hooking me up and you want to go again?"
ALEXIS: "Yup."
ME: "I gave you your minute earlier, now I need mine. I need some time to recover. Consumer demand is far outweighing production."

While waiting for my testes to produce more for Alexis to drink, I passed out for the night. I was surprised I didn't get rushed to the emergency room for having a lack of fluids.

At least I was able to make a 2.2 second contribution to her 10,000-hour rule. The bottom line was, I had achieved what I had initially set out to do in State College. Alexis placed me in a college state of mind. And I didn't mind.

Chapter 17

O-H-I-O, Ohio

Area 51 is a small patch of land located in America, that was often unrecognized on US maps. It is owned by the government and for years there was not much known about the place. It wasn't what people thought it was. Often times, perception is not reality. I found a similar situation when I went to a little know place. I will just refer to it as Oh-hi-ho, Ohio.

It was a Monday, and I was in the gym getting my daily workout routine in. That day I was working specifically on chest exercises. As I was laying on the bench press, I desperately tried pushing the weighted barbell away from my chest like it is was a 300-pound woman hovering me trying to get me to eat her sweet potato pie. While holding my breath and my face transforming to a bright red, I racked my weight.

My workout partner, JB was right there to spotting me. I sat up in order to rest in between sets.

JB: "How was your weekend?"

ME: "It was okay, nothing special. I just get sick of the same thing every weekend."

JB: "The same thing?"

ME: "You know, spending time getting dressed up, then going out to hit on women. Eventually, you see the same people every weekend. I need some sort of change. I see the same women. It's like they get passed around like a blunt."

By now, JB and I had switched places and I became his spotter as he did a few reps.

JB: "The problem is you're not expanding your horizons. Even horses get tired of drinking out of the same watering hole. Tell me one person in this world that eats at the same restaurant? Even though I love hamburgers I don't get them all the time at McDonald's. Sometimes I go to Burger King, or Wendy's."

ME: "And what do you suggest?"

JB: "You ever tried this whole online dating thing?"

ME: "Online dating?"

JB: "You know-eHarmony, Match.com, shit like that."

ME: "Nope. That kinda stuff is only for guys who are perverts and freaks."

JB: "Which means you would fit right in!"

I happily gave JB the birdie. I lay back on the bench to complete my next set of bench press. JB continues to spot me.

JB: "Wes, what type of women…do…you…think are online?"

ME: "They are only desperate women who can't get a man."

JB: "And what do lonely desperate women like to do? They don't sit at home knitting yarn."

I finished another set and racked the weights.

ME: "True. But, I can get a woman, anywhere. I don't need that online crap."

Magically, an attractive Persian girl in all black spandex was listening to her iPod and walked right in front us. Her booty smiled at me, and I didn't hesitate to smile back.

ME: "Let me show you how it's done. FYI this is without some eHarmony account. Take notes bitch!"

I hurried over and caught up to where there the woman was walking. I tried to get her attention from where I was.

ME: "Excuse me."

I could hear her music blasting in her ears from where I was standing. I tapped her on the shoulder and she quickly turned around. She yanked her white headphone out of her ear.

PERSIAN GIRL: "Yes?"
ME: "I don't want to interfere with your workout, but I just have to ask...Are you single?"
PERSIAN GIRL: "I am, and I want to keep it that way. Thanks."

The woman placed her headphone back in her ear and kept it moving. Meanwhile, I walked back to JB with my tail between my legs.

> **ME:** "What was the name of that site again?"
> **JB:** "Match.com. You have to trust me on this one. There will be plenty of women on there you can blaze. Most of the women on there say they want a relationship but in reality, they are all sluts ready to be dicked down. If you can't get laid on Match, you can't get laid anywhere."

Later that night, I contemplated what JB said. I think the fact that I got denied earlier that day influenced me to give it a try. The problem with creating an account on Match.com is that you have to come up with some creative bullshit to say. Even in cyberspace, you have to tell women what they want to hear. All women enjoy some sort of romance. Online dating is like jumping into an enormous lake. The water might not look the best, but your dick is guaranteed to get wet.

In order to save time, I looked up a random man's profile that lived clear across the country. Like a kindergartner in art class, I gave forth my best effort and did a copy and paste. Copied some other guy's romantic lies and pasted it on my page. Within five minutes my profile was up and running like a Kenyan marathon runner.

After a few hours, I was getting hits like a blunt at a Jamaican birthday party. However, every girl that was trying to interact with me was either big and beautiful or so unattractive that I wasn't certain if they were responding to my profile or RSVPing to a Monster's Ball.

Don't get me wrong, there is nothing wrong with ugly chicks, because I have definitely lowered my standards before, but messing with these women would have been borderline beastality. A lot of these women were sending me wink after wink.

A wink on Match.com is something an individual can send to another member to let them know they are interested in the other member. It provides a means to break the ice. Any woman I saw online that was smackable I would send a wink to.

It was a numbers game. The more winks I sent out the greater my chance to get a response. I didn't bother reading any of the profiles. Who has time for that? Reading online profiles are similar to preschoolers reading a storybook. Nobody cares what the words say, they just want to look at the pictures and eventually go out and play.

I was ready to play after seeing all of the profiles online. I was energized that all I had to do was wink at thousands of girls and could get return winks. This was a whole new experience for me.

I was faithful every night in doing wink exercises on Match.com. Skinny girl, wink. Big tittie girl, wink. Pretty smile, wink. The cross-eyed girl with coke-bottle glasses, wink. The girl I wouldn't dare be seen in a public even if she begged me...no way! On the contrary, she did look like she could suck a soccer ball through a stir straw. Wink!

The following week, as I was getting ready to log off my account for the night, I received a return wink from Elana. Judging by the pictures on Elana's profile, was she not only a cutie with a booty; she was thicker than a Snicker.

She seemed like a good wholesome girl. She had an innocent look about her and a warm smile. I wrote her in order to intro-

duce myself. She immediately responded and told me a little bit about her. We interacted on the site for a few days, and then we exchanged numbers.

When I finally called her, I noticed her voice matched her picture. She had a soft and soothing voice. I could tell this girl was down to earth and a good woman. We would talk for hours on the phone and had a lot of similar interests.

She was unique from most women. She was the type of woman that you settle down with and have a beautiful family with. What I gathered from our conversations was that she came from a good family; she was interested in a long-term relationship and loved to cook.

Moreover, she was a 6'0" and played volleyball player for The Ohio State University. She was sounding better and better by the minute. So much so, that I was thinking that she might be the one.

I got excited every time I saw her calling and had yet to meet her in person. Was I falling in love with this woman? Only time would tell. I am not the type to fall so quickly but she was sweeping me off of my feet.

What stood out from our phone communications was that she never said a curse word. Then one day I asked her about it.

ME: "Elana, I'm just going to flat out ask you. Do you ever cuss?"

ELANA: "No, not really. I have before but you have to get me really mad and something may slip. Good girls don't have to use foul language. My parents taught me to be lady-like."

ME: "Really? I've never met a girl like you. I admire that. I can't wait to meet you in person."
ELANA: "I'm anxious to meet you too!"

I was beginning to get butterflies. She was saying all the right things, I was counteracting with all the right things. Although Elana lived hours away, I couldn't wait any longer to see her.

ME: "So do I get an invite to see you?"
ELANA: "What took you so long to ask? Whenever you are ready, you can meet me."

My mouth responded before I could think about what I said.

ME: "I'm ready now."

Elana was a little taken aback by my statement.

ELANA: "What? Now? It is eight o' clock at night. You would not get here till late."
ME: "I was just playing...unless you're going to let me come."

There was a long pause over the phone.

ELANA: "I have workouts in the morning; I don't think it is a good idea. Plus it is a little late."
ME: "I understand..."
ELANA: "But, I do really want to see you! If you're serious, I will text you my address."

ME: "Send me that text, and I'll see you soon."
ELANA: "You're not serious, but I will text you anyway."

I hung up the phone and knew that Elana didn't think I was serious. However, I love to prove people wrong. Sure enough, Elana send me a text followed by a message doubting that I would come all the way out there. Ten minutes later I was in my car on my way to Columbus, Ohio.

I was so ecstatic; I immediately called JB.

ME: "Remind me to never doubt you!"
JB: "And why is that?"
ME: "I once doubted you about that site Match.com. Well, right now, I am on my way to meet my future wife in Columbus, Ohio."
JB: "Future wife? What are you talking about? You are driving all the way out there for some pussy? You can just get pussy around here."
ME: "Yeah, but this is no ordinary girl. She is a good girl, knows how to carry a conversation, and get this...she doesn't even cuss!"
JB: "Let me know how the pussy is!"
ME: "JB, I'm not going there for that. This isn't the kind of girl you have sex with on the first night. Trust me when I tell you this; she is different."
JB: "What did I tell you before? All girls on Match.com are sluts. You even said yourself to remind you to never doubt you! Well, I'm reminding you...don't doubt me!"

ME: "I beg to differ. This is an exception. I'm an expert in character and she is an amazing girl. I'm not going to let your jaded perspective ruin my evening. I'll call you when I leave from her house 'cause I know she is not going to let me stay the night."

JB: "Suit yourself; let me know how that goes..."

I got off of the phone with JB and was somewhat disappointed. Did he not believe in love anymore? Was he just hating on this great woman I discovered? After signing up for Match.com, I found out later that thousands of people found their spouses from the site. It happened to them, why not me?

Subsequent to my drive, I had finally made it to Elana's place. She seemed taller and prettier in person. She gave me a hug like I was a soldier coming home from the war. Her place was spotless and she had scented candles burning. It was obvious she cleaned her place inside and out just before I had arrived.

ELANA: "Welcome to my place. It is so good to finally meet you!"

I walked over and sat on her couch.

ELANA: "Can I offer you anything to eat or drink? I would offer you some wine but I don't drink. I did make some casserole earlier."

Domesticated, down to earth, pretty and athletic. I think we have a winner. I was beginning to hear wedding bells in my head.

ME: "Water is fine; thank you."

Elana went to the kitchen grabbed me a bottle of water and brought it back to where I was sitting. We continued to talk for another hour. I didn't want the night to end but I started to get somewhat sleepy.

ELANA: "You seem a little tired."

I admitted the obvious.

ME: "Yeah, a little."
ELANA: "Aww. It really means a lot that you came over here to see me tonight. You deserve a massage."

Elana reached over and started rubbing my neck and shoulders. I sat back and let her give one of the best massages of my life.

ME: "You have skills! Where did you learn how to give such great backrubs?"
ELANA: "I learned from our athletic trainers. The volley-ball team is always getting treatment and they massage our shoulders. I learned a lot from them."

I was about to fall asleep, so I cut my massage short.

Me: "I'm getting a little tired; I think it is best I get back on the road and head back. Thanks for everything. It was great meeting you."

I stood up and got my things together. Elana, being the selfless person she is, didn't want me driving back so late.

ELANA: "Wes, I'm really worried that you might fall asleep
while driving back. Why don't you just take a nap and
leave first thing in the morning."

Elana was so sweet she offered to share her bed with me.

ELANA: "Just so you know, you can sleep in my bed on one
condition."
ME: "What's that?"
ELANA: "I'm sleeping under the covers and you are sleep-
ing on top. I don't want you rubbing anything on me when
I'm trying to sleep."

I agreed and just thought the *World of Elana.* The more I was around
her, the more I enjoyed the things she did. JB was completely wrong
about this girl. He was clueless and didn't know quality when he saw it.

We made it to the bed and she turned the lights out. The
room was quiet like a library and I began dozing off.

Elana's voice woke me up.

ELANA: "Wes...are you awake?"
ME: "Barely. What's up?"
ELANA: "Why didn't you try and kiss me tonight? Are you
not attracted to me?"
ME: "Oh, no, I'm very attracted."

Elana positioned herself over to me and gave me the most innocent
peck on the lips. I returned the gesture and gave her a peck on
the lips.

ME: "Goodnight, I had fun with you tonight."

Instead of getting a goodnight response, Elana got out from under the covers and positioned herself in a straddled position on top of me. Her next actions surprised me somewhat. She aggressively started kissing me. It was like she was trying to do CPR on a conscious victim.

She went for my neck and was kissing it repeatedly like Woody Wood Pecker. Elana let out a moan and grabbed my right hand. She placed it on her breast as she began to grind on me. Then she suddenly stopped.

> **ELANA:** "I'm so horny, right now, I need to stop this. I don't want you thinking I'm a hoe."
> **ME:** "We aren't even doing anything. Why would I think you were a hoe? Just be yourself. That's you have to do. It's just me in here."
> **ELANA:** "Are you sure? You're not going to think that I am a hoe for letting you stay over, right?"
> **ME:** "I'm positive. Clearly you are a wonderful girl."
> **ELANA:** "You really think so?"
> **ME:** "I know so..."

Elana started kissing me again, this time with more passion and greater force than before. She reached back and cupped my balls like a jock strap. Next, she grabbed my shirt and violently took it off.

> **ELANA:** "I want you to FUCK me, right now!"
> **ME:** "Excuse me?"

She demanded my dick as if she was declaring war on it.

ELANA: "I want this Dick, and I want you to fuck me now."
ME: "Wait...I thought you didn't cuss?"
ELANA: "Damn it, Wes!"
ME: "But..."

Elana yanked my pants down so quickly, I didn't have time to react. It was all one motion. Then, Elana started giving me head like a two-headed monster. If I didn't know any better, I could have sworn there were two women giving me head down there.

ELANA: "I told you before; I only cuss when I get mad."
ME: "And you're mad at me?"
ELANA: "I'm mad you didn't give me this dick earlier."

After a few minutes she did like an ocean mammal and came up for air.

ELANA: "I'm ready to fuck now."

I was in utter shock. She went Pearl Harbor on my Donald Pump. She attacked it with no notice whatsoever.

ELANA: "So you're not going to think I'm loose right?"

Once I got past the surprise attack my Niagara Balls, I grabbed my Ohio State Buckeye and went volleyball on her enchilada of love. I gave it a few bumps, sets, and spikes.

ME: "No, not all! You are still a wonderful girl. Wonderful personality, wonderful head, and wonderful pussy."

ELANA: "Oh, like it when you talk shit to me."

My pork chop was moving back and forth in her applesauce. When all of a sudden, I got that tingling feeling like I was about to spill my milk. I had been working on the railroad and Dinah was about to blow. I gave Elana a heads up.

ME: "This thing is about to skeet; it's going to skeet!"

Elana pushed me off of her.

ELANA: "No wait, don't do it...not yet!"

Elana grabbed my Chief of Staff and placed it near her neck.

ELANA: "I want it all over my chest; come give it to me."

Next, my giving tree started giving...and giving...and giving a little more all over Elana's body.

I must say, Elana was one happy camper. When it was all said and done, she went back to the sweet innocent girl I knew. She offered to grab me water and another massage.

The next morning I had a long drive back from Ohio. I picked up my cell phone and called JB.

He answered the phone in a groggy voice.

JB: "Do you know what time it is? Half of the world is still sleep."

ME: "I called because, well... I owe you an apology."

JB: "Apology for what?"

ME: "Forgive me for ever doubting you!"

JB: "I don't get it."

ME: "Let me put it to you like this...If you can't get laid on Match.com, you can't get laid anywhere."

I thought Elana was something that she wasn't. In the end, JB was right about her. I guess we all have our misjudgments when evaluating character. On the bright side, not only was it fun while it lasted but I had fun while I was trying to last.

From now on, when one particular Midwestern state is mentioned in everyday conversations, most individuals hear it as Ohio. On the contrary, I hear the same state mentioned and can't help but think about when Elana blew me and my mind. Ohio will forever be remembered to me as Oh-hi-ho.

Similar to Area 51, I had discovered a place that wasn't well known. So if you ever run into any shy introverted women while visiting the great state of Ohio, beware. You might find yourself in Oh-hi-ho, Ohio.

Chapter 18

Forbidden Fruit

Parker ran a nonprofit organization for youth baseball players which contained over one hundred kids. Every year he threw an annual Holiday party. The great thing about a youth baseball holiday party is that there is a plethora of MILFS. I'm talking overabundance.com.

I had been recovering from foot surgery and was watching television on the couch. My foot was in a surgical boot propped up on the coffee table. My phone rang and it was Parker on the other line. I could hear loud music and laughter in the background.

> **PARKER:** "Dude! Where are you? There are a handful of hotties at this party!"
>
> **ME:** "What party?"
>
> **PARKER:** "Come on, I have been telling you about it all week! Come over. Quit feeling sorry for yourself. You have been on that couch all week. You're going to have fun. There are a whole bunch of hot moms here."

I got off the phone and started getting ready. There is one thing that is guaranteed to get a lazy man to rise from the couch; the

potential of getting his molten mushroom wet. Once I arrived to the party, there was a lot going on. There were people everywhere and the partygoers fluctuated in age.

It was as if there were two parties going on. The kids were mainly inside of the house, while the adults were mingling in the backyard. The kids were preoccupied inside of the house because they were all having a video game tournament. They were sipping on punch and eating homemade cookies.

On the other hand, the outside party was little more extravagant. The DJ was playing "Unchained Melody" by the Righteous Brothers. Hors d'oeuvres and champagne glasses were being passed around like a two-dollar whore. I walked toward the bar and sat down at one of the barstools. I was angry with myself for even coming to the party. I wanted to send out my own funeral invitations because I knew I was going to die of boredom.

A Jillian Michaels look-alike spotted me from the dance floor while I was sitting on a bar stool. Her eyes squinted and she zeroed in on me. She was noticeably a little buzzed from the champagne. This gave her more courage to get what she wanted: me. Boldly she walked over, grabbed my hand and started yanking my arm like a limp dick in the heat of passion.

MILF: "Come dance with me!"
ME: "No, thanks. I am fine right here. Plus I recently had surgery on my foot."
MILF: "Quit being a bum. I have been watching you all night and you have been sitting in this same spot. You hear this music? Don't let these songs go to waste."

Soon after she started pulling my arm as if it were a limp dick, she started talking to me as if I was a limp dick.

> **MILF:** "Get up! Come 'on! You need to get up."

I tried to stall and change the subject.

> **ME:** "I'm sorry. I didn't catch your name. But of course it's hard to catch anything when I'm being blinded by that huge rock on your hand."
> **MILF:** "Colleen."

With her hand still glued to my arm, I finally stood up.

> **ME:** "Where is your husband? Why isn't he dancing with you? I'm not trying to get beat up by a jealous husband at a kid's holiday party."
> **COLLEEN:** "Trust me you have nothing to worry about. We are just dancing and my husband has seen me dance with other people."

Colleen quickly changed the subject from her husband to the cup I was holding.

> **COLLEEN:** "You're drinking water, which means that you constantly like to be aware of your surroundings. You don't like a lot of drama and are somewhat health conscious. And judging by the way you are holding your cup, you like to be in control."

ME: "You're telling me that you picked all of that up from me holding a cup of water?"

COLLEEN: "Yep. I'm what you would call a drink connoisseur. I've studied social behavior and contextual clues that people give off in social settings."

Colleen broke down social behaviors associated with other drinks such as wine, beer and various types of beverages.

ME: "How do you know all of this? Did you major in social drinking?"

COLLEEN: "I'm a former CIA agent. I stalked people for a living. I was paid to people watch. I would often sit at random diners across the world and act like I was tourist. My partner would act as my husband, pretending we were on a honeymoon. I would pretend I was taking pictures of him but in reality, I would aim the camera, over his shoulder and take photos of our target."

My mind was blown like the consequence of a fatal suicide.

ME: "Now, that is what I call a job!"

COLLEEN: "It wasn't all cracked up as it sounds. It was boring most of the time. Just following random people and then nothing would become of it. It wasn't like the way it's depicted in the movies."

ME: "Why did you get out of it?"

COLLEEN: "My husband wanted me to stay home and watch the kids. He still works for the agency while I take care of the kids."

ME: "Since, I'm out here dancing with you, I am not going to get shot, my body never to be seen again, am I?"

COLLEEN: "No, no, no. As I told you before, my husband is out of the country."

ME: "But couldn't he get access to all of your phone records, Internet searches, and all that?"

COLLEEN: "I'm sure he could with good reason."

Three songs had passed, and Colleen was already playing grab ass. She kept squeezing both of my booty cheeks like they were stress balls.

COLLEEN: "You have such a nice ass. If I wasn't married, we would be having a lot of fun."

ME: "You're not having fun now?"

COLLEEN: "I am, but if I wasn't married, we would probably leave this party a little early and finish the night back at my place."

Colleen was kind of like a rental car. You wouldn't mind taking it for a spin for the day and riding it rough. However, you knew you had to turn it back in to its rightful owner after putting a few extra miles on it. It was apparent that Colleen loved to work out. She was in her mid to late forties and had an ass like an apple. Since she was married, however, her apple was forbidden fruit.

Like anal sex, the night came to an end. I didn't even try to close the deal with a phone number. Even though I left with a piece of mind, I could tell Colleen wanted to get piece of mine. I had refused to take a bite from the forbidden fruit.

The following week, I got a call from a local number that I failed to recognize. It was a sexy woman's voice on the other line.

WOMAN'S VOICE: "Hi! Wes?"
ME: "Yes...who is this?"

Woman's voice:"This is Colleen from the holiday party. Remember me? I was the only person able to peel you off the bar stool that you were glued to."

ME: "I remember. How did you get my number?"
COLLEEN: "Where there is a will, there is a way."

The fact that Colleen was able to get my number was somewhat suspect. She was displaying early characteristics of a stalker. To this day, I still don't know how Colleen got my number and she refused to tell me. It has always been her little secret. Since she was an attractive MILF, I just went along with it.

Colleen reminded me of a classic car. Although it was built before you were born, everyone loved to look at it. You also wanted to know what it was like in the inside, even though you knew it had been around the block a few times.

COLLEEN: "I had a few minutes before I had to pick my kids up from school and wanted to know if you could meet me for lunch."

I was flattered that this woman was inviting me to lunch so I agreed. We met up for lunch at her favorite Greek restaurant. The lunch

was as innocent as a suspect pleading guilty with no evidence left unturned. She was flirting with me the whole time.

The lunch dates went on for a few weeks. I could tell that Colleen was starting to get emotionally invested. She would reveal things about her marriage; it was falling apart and she always felt neglected at home. She was a desperate housewife.

Colleen would call me every day after her husband left for work and she dropped the kids off to school. The worse thing about the whole situation was that she lived in my neighborhood and her best friend Sharon, lived a few houses down from me.

I was physically attracted to her, and over time, I saw her as a good friend. I wanted to taste the forbidden fruit but like an illegal immigrant, I knew I wasn't supposed to cross that line.

Early one morning, Colleen called me.

COLLEEN: "Happy birthday, big boy!"
ME: "Ah, you remembered my birthday! Thank you!"
COLLEEN: "What are you doing today?"
ME: "A few of my friends are taking me to dinner tonight and then we are going out later."
COLLEEN: "I need to see you today. I have a surprise for your birthday."

I was excited and grateful that Colleen thought about me on my birthday. It was icing on the cake that she had a surprise for me.

ME: "What is it?"
COLLEEN: "Well, I have to see you so I can give it to you. Are you busy now?"

ME: "No, I was about to watch some TV."
COLLEEN: "Come over, I am house sitting for Sharon right down the street."
ME: "Where is Sharon?"
COLLEEN: "They went on a vacation and will be back next week. My husband took the kids to the zoo today and I have to meet up with them in a bit. I told them I would meet at them zoo because he had to take my son to his baseball game. Anyway, hurry up, and come over before your surprise gets cold."
ME: "I'll be right over."

I eagerly left my place with a pep in my step and walked down to Sharon's house. I feared that my surprise was going to get cold. I hurried as fast as I could. There is nothing worse than eating a home cooked meal that grows cold. I like my food just like I like my women; hot and smelling good.

I rang the doorbell and anxiously awaited my surprise.

Colleen opened the door and let me in. Next, she embraced me with a sensual hug.

COLLEEN: "I wanted to be one of the people that you spent your special day with."

Colleen gave me a light kiss on the cheek.

I tried to anticipate what she may have been cooking on the stove. I took a whiff of the air only to find out that my sense of smell was only detecting the aroma of her sweet perfume. Somewhat confused, I walked in the kitchen and inquired about my surprise.

ME: "I rushed over here, because you said my surprise was getting cold."

COLLEEN: "It was getting cold. Stay right there; I need to go get it."

Colleen scurried out of the kitchen as I waited with my back leaned against the kitchen counter. Colleen was gone for about five minutes. The anticipation was rattling my brain and I grew impatient.

ME: "Hello? Are you still in here?"

Colleen yelled from the next room.

COLLEEN: "OK, close your eyes and count to ten."

I closed my eyes tight, and was expecting a fancy cake with candles.

ME: "One, two, three, four..."

I could hear Colleen's voice grow closer to me.

COLLEEN: "Are they closed? You're not cheating are you?"

ME: "No! I have 'em closed."
COLLEEN: "Okay, open! Surprise!"

I open my eyes and my surprise was glaring right at me. Colleen stood in front of me wearing a white satin strapless corset with garters and a G-string. My regurgitator of rsejuvenation started

expanding and trying to break through my zipper. I took a 7-Eleven sized big gulp.

COLLEEN: "Happy birthday!"

Colleen walked towards me with her lips puckered out like she was trying to kiss me. I resisted her kiss by pushing her off of me.

ME: "Thank you! But you said my surprise was getting cold."
COLLEEN: "I'm the surprise. I was getting cold. I even wore your favorite color. You can give it to me right here and right now."
ME: "But you are married...I can't."

As I hesitated, she made me say verbatim her prior employer's name without me even realizing it.

ME: "See, I..."

She grabbed my crotch.

ME: "Aye!"

She moved in closer and started kissing my neck. As she kissed my neck and felt up my chest, my conscious had an argument with itself. It was Good Wes vs. Bad Wes.

GOOD WES: "What are you doing? She is married; you have never been with a married woman. Plus you met her at a youth event. Be a role model for kids."

BAD WES: "It never matters how or where people meet. What really counts is when your little member is doing one armed pushups inside of a dark tunnels until it reaches the point at which he is forced to vomit."

Colleen unbuckled my belt and pulled my pants down, just enough to show penis cleavage.

GOOD WES: "Stop while you're ahead! It's not too late. You are going to break up a happy home. You can't send her the zoo with dick on her breath. Get out of the house! Abort the mission!"
BAD WES: "Look here, all she wants to do is probably spit shine the little German war helmet. It's only head; it's not really cheating."

I had made up my mind. I wasn't going to do it. Call me a sucker. I needed to have some dignity about the situation. It was all-wrong. I could never live with the fact that she would do the mess around with me, and then kiss her beautiful children when she saw them. With my mind made up I reached down to pull my sagging pants up.

She saw what I was trying to do and instead of letting me go free, she stripped my pants down like an '82 Chevy caprice going in for a paint job. Next, I heard the call of the wild. The entire making up my mind and moral shit went out of the window. She was acting like it was the first day of spring and her pussy was coming out of hibernation. While her husband was at the zoo with the kids, she made me feel as if I was at the zoo with her.

She started grabbing for my elephant trunk as I glanced at her camel toe. Then she started spanking my monkey. So I reached over and felt her duck-billed platypus. I assumed she was sporting a bald eagle, but when she pulled her panties off, she revealed a tiger stripe. Her beef curtains looked like a stingray.

> COLLEEN: "I have more surprises to give you. Tell me how you like this..."

As I was still leaning against the counter, like a polar bear she went down on my north pole. Giving me long neck like a giraffe. She was giving me that Gorilla head; the kind that will make Tarzan beat his chest. This caused my foot to move like tail of a rattlesnake. All I could think about was her alligator snapper.

I picked her up on put her on the kitchen counter. Her legs opened up like the wings from a monarch butterfly. She pulled me close and wrapped her hand around my chicken like a boa constrictor. I started giving her my milk snake.

Colleen had some good octopus. I was trying to save my little tadpoles like they were an endangered specifies. I didn't want them escaping too early. In the middle of it all, I felt like an unfaithful Muslim, because I knew I shouldn't have been porking. I felt like a vulture, I was enjoying a meal that wasn't mine. After a few minutes her pelican had my squinty Blow Pop spitting like a llama.

While I was still out of breath and trying to gather myself, Colleen's phone started ringing. We both looked at each other standing naked like Adam and Eve in the Garden of Eden. She looked down at the caller ID.

COLLEEN: "Shit, it's my husband."

She grabbed the phone and answered.

> **COLLEEN:** "Hi, Hun. Yes, I am still at Sharon's house. Did
> Jason win his game? That's great! Well, I am just wrapping
> it up over here at Sharon's. I am just going to wipe the
> counter off cause I spilled some juice then I'll head down...
> ok...got it...love you too. Bye!"

Colleen hung up the phone and I gave her a look as if I couldn't
believe what she had said.

> **COLLEEN:** "What? I didn't lie! We wrapped it up over here,
> and I am going to wipe that counter. I can't have Sharon
> eating from the counter, when I had sex juices all over it."

Colleen wiped the counter down, we got in her car and she dropped
me off down the street. The rest of my birthday was a blur. I had
just screwed a former CIA agent that was currently married to a
CIA agent. That is the quickest way to come up missing.

I was paranoid for the next few months, constantly looking over
my shoulder. I kept having nightmares that her husband would use
interrogation tactics so I would confess to hitting the pussy.

After my birthday, Colleen's calls became less and less frequent until they eventually stopped. Either she felt guilty about the
situation or she just moved onto the next guy. Regardless, I took a
bite of the forbidden fruit and made apple pie with it. She brought
the cake and I came with the icing. Happy birthday to me.

Chapter 19

Why The Tooth Fairy Went Bankrupt

As a child I can vividly remember the first time I lost a tooth. My mother sat me down and told me all about the Tooth Fairy. She told me to put my tooth under my pillow. I was somewhat skeptical at first but I complied and went to sleep that night. When I woke up, *Viola! Magic.* There was a nickel under my pillow.

I was rich. I was amazed that some fairy could come in the middle night and give me cash for my pearly whites. From that point on, I was constantly wiggling teeth and checking them to see if any were loose. As I grew older, I would often look forward to the day when a tooth would fall out.

Then like clockwork, I would place a tooth under my pillow and wake up richer. I experienced gains of 25% each time I lost a tooth. My financial portfolio was increasing at a rapid rate. The more teeth that came out of my mouth, the more my cash payments increased.

I started out earning a nickel for every tooth, then they eventually increased to a dollar for every tooth. At this rate, I just knew I would become a millionaire one day. I came to the conclusion that all my parents had to do was put their missing teeth under

their pillows and the family would be filthy rich. At their age, I esti-mated they should have been getting at least one-hundred dollars a tooth.

One day I was having pipe dreams of becoming a billionaire tycoon from exporting my own teeth. Until one day my mother broke the bad news to me. She informed me that once my baby teeth left, then my permanent teeth will grow back in. The new set are the only new teeth I will ever get. I was devastated.

Reality had slapped me in the face. There was a reason why my family wasn't making billions from tooth sales. I knew that once all my baby teeth fell out, the Tooth Fairy would only come if and only if my permanent teeth fell out. I felt as though I was get-ting the shit end of the stick.

Nevertheless, the situation made me that more appreciative when the Tooth Fairy left me money. One night, while I only had a few baby teeth left, I happened to lose another tooth. Once again, I was thrilled at the opportunity of making more money. So I con-tinued with the same routine, pulled the tooth and tucked it under my pillow.

I woke up the next morning, extended my arm beneath the pillow and found…nothing. No tooth, no money. I slid out from underneath the covers and looked under my bed. Nothing. I thought to myself that may have dropped my money. I frantically lifted up my pillow one more time and double-checked the bottom of my pillow. I concluded that The Tooth Fairy took my tooth and left me no money.

Questions began formulating over and over in my head. I con-tinued to contemplate the same three questions and put them on repeat like your favorite song on the radio.

QUESTION 1: Did the Tooth Fairy forget to leave me my money?

QUESTION 2: Did the Tooth Fairy steal from me?

QUESTION 3: Did the Tooth Fairy run out of money?

I knew that the Tooth Fairy didn't forget to leave me money because she left all the other kids in my classroom money whenever she came to visit them. I was certain the Tooth Fairy didn't steal from me because I never thought fairies could be that cold hearted. So it left me with the conclusion that the Tooth Fairy simply ran out of money.

I decided that since the Tooth Fairy had been so generous in the past with giving me money, that I would give her a pass. I was going to give her one-week to come up with the payment. If she didn't give me my money, we were going to have problems.

I was angry inside and wanted to give the Tooth Fairy a piece of my mind. Throughout the week, I started asking my friends if anyone had a phone number or address so I could find her. Nobody knew *anything*. She was like a ghost in the wind. The Tooth Fairy scammed me.

Throughout the week, I faithfully checked underneath my pillow. Time after time, day after day, I was let down. Once the week ended, I made an assumption that the Tooth Fairy was not paying me because she ran out of cash.

Bankruptcy occurs when a person is unable to pay their debts to their respective creditors. The Tooth Fairy was bankrupt. The bitch couldn't pay her bills anymore. Although I didn't understand

the term "bankruptcy" back then, I was aware that people sometimes were unable to pay what they owed.

What I did understand was that the Tooth Fairy never paid
me what she owed. Therefore, I hated her after that. I vowed to
one day figure out why the Tooth Fairy went bankrupt. Years later,
I finally got my answer.

Present Day

With the success rate I was having at Match.com, I started to
become addicted to it. Every woman that wrote me provided a
new challenge. Women were throwing themselves at me like slow
pitch softball. I was having trouble keeping track, because the women
were issuing numbers faster than a prison warden. It's like walking
into an all-you-can-eat buffet when your stomach is full. You love
what's on the menu, but it's still difficult to consume anything else.

One particular girl stood out from the rest of the women
only because I had never heard of the city listed in her profile. She
was from a place called Derry, Pennsylvania. Derry is the equivalent to what an Asian penis is in the sex world. It is known for
being so small some people fail to realize even there.

The biggest retail store they have near Derry is a Wal-Mart,
which is in the next town over. The fanciest five-star restaurant
they have in Derry is what people refer to as a McDonald's.

Gale initiated contact with me.

Her message read: Hello, I wanted to introduce myself. My
name is Gale and I wanted to let you know that I think you one
of the sexiest men on match. I would like to get to know you
better ;)

When Gale told me I was one of the sexiest men on Match.com, my ego was stroked like it had just come out of a Chinatown massage parlor. I wrote back, introduced myself and told her we should meet up soon.

Within minutes she wrote me back and told me she was down to meet me. She told me a little bit about herself. She told me that she ran a cookie business out of her house and would bake the cookies then sell them to the local residents.

Five days and seven email exchanges later, I was on my way out to State College, Pennsylvania, so we decided to meet up at the local Wal-Mart near Derry. I took the opportunity to see if her profile represented her true self.

Gale arrived at Wal-Mart shortly before I did. When we met up, she was already pushing a full cart of groceries. She looked somewhat similar to the pictures on her profile, however, her mannerisms were a little strange.

GALE: "Wes, it's so nice to finally meet you."

Gale leaned over and gave me the biggest hug. Soon after our intimate hug, she started looking around in every direction in a paranoid manner as if someone was following her.

I seemed to catch her off guard as she was looking past my shoulder.

ME: "Did you just see an ex- boyfriend or something?"
GALE: "Huh? Um no, I'm fine."
ME: "What are you looking at? And why are you so fidgety?"

Gale started grinding her teeth.

> **GALE:** "I'm fine; I'm just in a hurry to get back and make
> my cookies."
> **ME:** "Don't let me hold you up. I have to leave as well. It
> was good to finally meet you."

Our interaction was brief and with that, I gave Gale a hug and left the store. That was the first and last time I expected to see Gale. That is, until I got a text from Gale two hours later while driving in my car.

> **GALE:** "It was so nice meeting you. You are an extremely
> sexy man. So sexy that I couldn't help myself and had a
> mini photo shoot with myself. Hope you like my picture."

Attached to the text message was a picture of Gale in her bra. When I saw this, I pushed it to the limit, which began an exchange of text messages.

> **ME:** "Where are the rest of the pics? You're holding out
> on me."
> **GALE:** "I have more but I don't know if you can handle
> them. They are much sexier…I even took videos. I don't
> want to scare you."
> **ME:** "Send them! I doubt you will scare me. I know what I
> can handle…"

Like true super hoe, Gale sent me four different pictures. Each picture downloaded one at time.

PICTURE 1: Gale was standing in her black bra and matching black panties.

PICTURE 2: Gale was now standing in her black panties. The bra was like an open gift under the Christmas tree on December 26th. It was no longer present.

PICTURE 3: Gale is lifting up her left breast with one hand. She is licking her nipple like a postal stamp.

PICTURE 4: Gale's panties had disappeared. All that was left showing was her paraphernalia.

The first thought that crossed my mind was that Gale was going to be a lot like a game of tee-ball, a guaranteed hit.

I responded with a sarcastic text.

ME: "You don't scare me, Casper. It is going to take much more than a few G-rated photos to get me excited."
GALE: "Oh, yeah?"

Another download was coming in to my phone. There was a message sent with the attachment.

GALE: "How is this for scare tactics?"

When the attachment opened, it was a close up of Gale holding her vibrator. She must have named it Alice, because it was all up in her Wonderland.

Without delay, I sent a text back.

ME: "You are so sexy and so right. I am scared now and my heart is racing! I am so frightened that I know I won't be able to sleep without you tonight."
GALE: "Aw poor baby. I knew you wouldn't be able to handle it. What's your address? I'll make sure we leave the night light on."

It was already getting late so I sent Gale the address to my hotel and told her to meet me around eleven o'clock. Gale wasn't the prettiest girl in the world but I knew beauty was only a light switch away. Gale was one of the girls that fell under the "no snitching" category. A girl you would smash but would never snitch and tell your friends. Everyone in the world has pussy they hit they weren't too proud of. Gale was one of those types.

At eleven sharp, I heard a knock on my hotel door. Gale had arrived right on schedule. When I opened the door she threw her arms around me as if she had known me for years.

GALE: "Hi, baby! It's so nice to see you again!"
ME: "Nice to see you, too!"

I threw a famous disclaimer out there as she entered my room.

ME: "I'm just letting you know you can't stay all night. I have to be up early. So we have an hour to hangout and do whatever it is we are going to do; then, you have to leave."

To the average girl, this statement might have turned her away, but with Gale, it only turned her on.

GALE: "I like you...you get straight to the point!"

It was obviously turning Gale on that I was upfront with her. I began asking her basic questions that I didn't really care the answer to. Such as how was her drive and what she wanted to be when she grew up. During our conversation, I noticed that Gale had a few molars on the side of her mouth that were rotten like last week's apples.

In the fight between enamel vs. cavity, the fight needed to be called off because cavity was winning by a landslide. There was no coming back from that. Clearly she had her own Thrilla in Manila going on in that yuck mouth. In her defense, she did have a few front teeth that seemed ok. They were good enough to not re-quire dentist attention.

Our conversation continued a mere five minutes until my phone started ringing. The commotion from my phone drew Gale's attention. She glanced over at my phone and happened to see my caller ID, which read Jolene.

GALE: "Oh, so who is Jolene?"

One thing I hate more than yuck mouth women are nosey yuck mouth women. Although I had no woman in my life at the time, I told her what she wanted to hear.

ME: "My girlfriend."
GALE: "Wes, you have a girlfriend?"

ME: "You have a toothbrush?"

GALE: "What? What are you talking about?"

ME: "Oh, I thought that we were talking about things that are irrelevant in each other's lives."

Gale got the point and stopped asking questions me dumb questions.

GALE: "Well...I was just trying to make conversation. Jeez! I'm sure she is a nice girl."

Gale was like a nearby convenience store when you're headed home at 3:00 am from the bar. You have no problems passing it up and just going straight to bed. However, since you're already there, you might as well stop in and get some.

Gale sat next to me on the bed. She started rubbing my shoulders, neck, and hands. Her hands got frisky like a TSA agent and began feeling all over me. Like Little Caesar's Pizza, Gale was hot and ready.

I placed her on the bed and started giving it to her. I was hitting her womb so good you would have thought I was trying to add a branch to my family tree. The problem was, her cuntry pie was barely moist which was a huge turn off for me.

Like a golfer, I had reached par and was ready to move on to the next hole.

ME: "I'm tired of putting in all this work. How about you just give me a lil' head?"

Gale eagerly obliged and flipped me over. She then went to town on my Pennis the Menace. Her head game was so good that in the

back of my head I was signing Drake's *The Best I Ever Had*. As she came up for air, I felt something fall on my pubic bone.

ME: "What in the..."

I peered over the horizon of my chest and looked down to see what was on my pubic area. With what I saw laying on top of me, even Chicken Little would have thought the sky was falling. I noticed a pair of pearly whites that had fallen down like the Berlin wall.

Gale quickly cupped her mouth with her hand in sheer embarrassment.

GALE: "Whoops."

It was evident. Gale had no teeth. Her fronts came out like Elton John in 1988. I was left with two options:

1. Ask her to continue sucking
2. Take my pacifier out of her mouth.

I was so disgusted of the possibly that she could be kissing my thunder stick with no teeth that I would never be able to live with myself. If my friends ever found out, I could never play it down that I received a gum job.

Nonetheless, my mom always taught me to see the positive in every situation. In that case, I didn't have to worry about her scraping my top. Gums are there for a reason, so I allowed her to put them to use.

ME: "Why'd you stop? Keep going."

Gale had no shame. She picked her teeth up and threw them to the side then continued her duties. Gale's teeth were a dying species with no resurrection date. I concluded that she must have smoked them. Meth is a hellava drug. Nevertheless, she eventually got me to spill my man milk down her esophagus.

ME: "Now that was some good head."

The smut was so proud that I had served her a protein shake.

GALE: "Thank you!"

I always wondered why old grandpas were so relaxed sitting around the house not having a care in the world. It's because the grandmas with no teeth are giving head like a champ. You do the math. If a grandma is 80 years old, and she has been giving head since she was 16, which is 64 years of perfecting oral sex. When you mix in no teeth and all gum, it's like having a tuned up engine with nitrous. You are working with something!

GALE: "I know you have to get up early, so I'm going to get going."

Gale popped her teeth back in her mouth and made her way out of my hotel room. I locked the door behind her and went back to bed. I turned out the lights and sat in my bed. I contemplated what had just happened and everything hit me at once.

If it weren't for Gale, my lifelong question would have never been answered. I now knew why the Tooth Fairy went bankrupt.

Gale was the missing link all of these years. If there weren't ratchet girls like Gale in the world then the Tooth Fairy could pay all of her debts.

Girls like Gale have been abusing the system losing more teeth than they should have. This causes the Tooth Fairy to pay out more money, leaving honest hard working tooth losers with nothing under their pillow. So if you are reading this and ever wondered as a child why the Tooth Fairy went bankrupt you can thank Gale.

Chapter 20

Famous Last Words

It was 5:00 am and I was heading back to my car from Kathy's house.

"You can come over, but don't think that I'm sleeping with you." That was the last definitive declaration I recalled hearing from Kathy six hours earlier.

I could only smile as I started my car's ignition. I had completely debunked her hypothesis. I came, after I saw and conquered. Kathy was like an ancient philosopher claiming the earth was flat. It sounded logical at the time but when it came down to it, but the statement was far from reality.

Kathy called me on the phone while driving.

KATHY: "I hope this just isn't going to be a onetime thing. I just don't want to be your *fuck buddy*."
ME: "How about you just be my buddy? Then, occasionally, when the stars align in my favor, we can fuck."
KATHY: "Isn't that what a fuck buddy is?"
ME: "I guess you're right. Well, you can stop being my buddy, and we can just fuck..."

Needless to say, that was the last time Kathy and I hooked up. We just became buddies. Similar to an unhappily married couple, the

fuck part was missing. I would sporadically hear from Kathy over the next few days. What I didn't anticipate is that Kathy's quote "don't think I'm sleeping with you" would be said to me in the future in a span of three days by four different women.

One evening I logged onto G-chat. I noticed Kathy's profile came up and her profile picture was with some guy showing off a ring on her left hand. Her display message read "Engaged and excited".

Instantaneously, I wrote Kathy.

ME: "You're engaged?"
KATHY: "Yes."

I picked up my phone and had to hear it from my own ears.

ME: "Congrats! I had no idea. So when did this happen? How long were you two together?"
KATHY: "We were on and off the past three years."
ME: "I see. So...when is the wedding?"
KATHY: "It's in August."
ME: "August? Why so soon?"
KATHY: "I know. I feel bad for not telling you any of this. You're a great guy and I like you a lot. I just wasn't sure where my relationship was going."
ME: "Apparently, it's going down the aisle."
KATHY: "Listen. I actually have someone that is very interested in you. I showed my friend a picture of you. This person has no idea that we ever hooked up. All they know is that you are one my good friends."

Ah, it's the gift that keeps on giving. Kathy had sacked my sac in the sack and was now pawning me off to one of her girlfriends.

> ME: "Oh, really? Which one of your girlfriends is this?"
> KATHY: "Well...it's not really one of my girlfriends."
> ME: "A guy? What kinda sick twisted girl are you?"
> KATHY: "Calm down. It's not a guy. Well it's..."
> ME: "Spit it out..."
> KATHY: "It's my younger sister."
> ME: "I'm sure we can make that work."

Kathy was pretty, but everyone around town was also familiar with her younger sister Katrina. Katrina was one of the best looking girls in the city. Katrina was like a shoplifter in Nordstrom, she stole all the good genes in that family.

I officially met Katrina a short time later through her sister, Kathy. Katrina and I hung out and went on a few dates but nothing transpired. It was if my sex game was constipated. I was putting everything into dates with Katrina and nothing was coming out.

With the wedding date being around the corner, I was invited to Kathy's wedding. Awkward, I know. What was even more awkward was the fact that Katrina and Kathy's parents allowed me to stay at their house for the wedding.

Thursday

I flew into Charlotte, North Carolina and attended Kathy's wedding as Katrina's date.

Their parents just thought that I was some new guy dating Katrina. They weren't aware that Kathy's eggs had come close to getting fertilized by yours truly.

Friday

It was somewhat awkward when I got introduced to the groom at the night wedding.

KATHY: "Wes, I want you to meet my husband, Lance."

I extended my hand.

LANCE: "Great to meet you, Wes. Oh, how do you two know each other?"

I wanted to blurt out, "Your wife used to give me sloppy toppy!" But instead I stayed silent and Kathy gave a quick explanation.

KATHY: "I met him through Katrina. Babe, he is Katrina's date tonight. They have been dating for a while. I told you about him but you must have been preoccupied."

Kathy avoided the awkwardness and took Lance by the hand and began walking in the opposite direction.

KATHY: "Let me introduce you to some of my friends from undergrad."

I went off looking for Katrina.

When the wedding was over, Katrina took me downtown to meet up with a few of her friends that she went to high school with back in the day. As the night went on, Katrina was throwing back drinks. She started loosening up a little bit.

I knew I had a chance to sex her up. A woman intoxicated is a lot like a microwave oven. All you have to do is push a few buttons and your meat will be left just how you like in only half the time.

> **KATRINA:** "Let's get out of her babe. I'm kind of tired. It's been a long day."

Although I was staying at her parents' house, Katrina was staying in the upstairs bedroom and I was staying downstairs in the guest bedroom. Once we arrived to the house, Katrina went in the kitchen and fixed herself a small snack.

I, on the other hand, went to the bedroom and checked my luggage to make certain that I had a rubber for my clubber. *Bingo!* I placed the rubber on the side of the bed so I could gain access to it later. Now that's what I refer to as great product placement.

As I walked back into the kitchen to meet up with a tipsy Katrina, I could hear her parents snoring upstairs. All I could think about was getting a quickie in while the parents were catching some Zs. When the cats are gone, the mice will play. I approached Katrina from behind and started kissing the back of her neck.

> **ME:** "Let's go back to my room and lie down."

Katrina removed both of my arms from around her waist. Next, I heard the same words that her sister had told me earlier that year.

KATRINA: "Just so you know, I'm not sleeping with you. I'm actually really tired. I am going to head to bed."
ME: "What do you mean you're just going to go to bed?"
KATRINA: "Just what I said."
ME: "But I fly out tomorrow. You don't want to hangout for a second?"
KATRINA: "Nope. I'm going upstairs. Have a goodnight."

Katrina leaned over gave me a kiss on my cheek and strutted up the stairs. Not only did she tell me she wasn't sleeping with me, she walked away after saying it. I had just been served a double dose of rejection. Feeling dusted and disgusted, I walked shamefully to my room and jumped in the bed.

I was doing *way* too much. I was naïve to think that I could sleep with two sisters. Those types of situations were mythical and only happened in pornos. I figured out quickly that I wasn't as good as I thought I was.

By now it was 3am and I my eyes were struggling to stay open like a car dealership in an Amish community. I shut off the light next to the bed and I was drooling on my pillow within minutes. I was in a deep sleep for hours.

I guess since I had spent all night with Katrina I started dreaming about her. I was awakened by a loud thud on my bed. Confused and disoriented I looked at the clock which read 5am.

ME: "What in the..."

Once I became aware of my surroundings, I looked over and lying next to me was Katrina. I guess dreams do come true.

ME: "Couldn't sleep?"
KATRINA: "No, not really."

Katrina scooted closer to me. The room was getting a little brighter from the sun about to come. I noticed that she was wearing only a nightgown. I reached around her waistline and also noticed she had no panties on.

It was obvious what she was in my bed for, and it wasn't for a bedtime story. Like a cameraman on a porn set, I could see this one coming.

Katrina started rubbing my inner thighs and grabbed my staff sergeant. She then proceeded to give me a hickey on my dickey. Next, I reached for my rubber and she eagerly jumped on top of me. We started having stealth sex.

Stealth sex is the art of having sex *without* making any noise. The couple must maintain a standard of silence, whereas not a peep is heard. Many young college students go through their college years mastering the art of stealth sex. It is a useful tool of survival when a young lad is trapped in a tiny dorm with one or two roommates.

We were at black belt level with our stealth sex. We were so quiet that I would have made my elementary school librarian happy. When we finally finished, Katrina snuck back to her room. Katrina had pulled off one of the greatest jewelry heists in history.

She crept past her parents, walked into an unsuspecting room and got to my family jewels. Personally, I felt like a tennis ball during a Serena and Venus Williams match, both sisters got to hit me.

I went back to sleep once again.

Saturday

When I finally woke up in the morning, Katrina's mom was in the kitchen cooking me breakfast while talking to Katrina.

> **KATRINA'S MOM:** "So did you two have fun last night? What did you guys do?"
> **KATRINA:** "We just laid low. Didn't do too much, we kept it quiet."

Katrina looked towards me and gave me a wink. It was our little secret. I was pleased like a kid with good manners.

When it was time for me to leave Charlotte that evening, Katrina dropped me off at the airport. At the time I was living in Pittsburgh, PA. Once on the plane, I reclined my chair back and giggled to myself as I thought about how Katrina and Kathy's statements were similar right before they slept with me. They made it a point to tell me that they weren't going to sleep with me.

I was so exhausted from the previous night that I hadn't realized I had fallen asleep until we were landing at my destination. While waiting for my luggage in baggage claim, JB called me.

> **JB:** "You trying to go out tonight?"

ME: "Naw."

JB: "Come on! I hear the freaks are going to be out tonight. Plus it's a full moon. Go ahead and come out so you can get your dick wet."

ME: "I'm just getting back in town from a wedding, and it's well past midnight. By the time I get my bags and get my car, it will be one o' clock. It's going to take me thirty minutes to get to a club. By then, it will be too late to get any girls. I'm going to get my bags and head straight home."

JB: "I'm telling you, you need to come out! What do you have to lose?"

ME: "OK, I'll meet you out. But...I'm not trying to stay out late."

JB: "Man, just bring your ass down to the S Bar!"

I drove straight from the airport to S Bar. S Bar is a club located in Pittsburgh's Southside where many of the Pittsburgh Steelers frequently attend. When the Steelers come out, the groupies quickly follow and swallow. The groupies are ready to pounce on any man that remotely resembles a football player.

By the time we got into S Bar, the club was going to shut down in thirty minutes. My window of opportunity was closing by the second and I was having an off night. The women weren't that into me for whatever reason. I grew frustrated and tired so I decided to leave. Meanwhile, JB was talking to this girl Raquel he had been trying to sleep with for the past three weeks.

I walked over to where the two were standing in order to say goodnight.

ME: "JB, I'm headed home. I need to get some rest; I have been up all day."

While talking to JB, Raquel grabbed him by the shoulder and whispered something in his ear.

JB then revealed what Raquel had told him.

JB: "She says her girl over there, wearing the blue top, is interested in you."
ME: "That's cool and all, but I'm going home. I'll walk over there and say hi so they don't think I'm rude."

I went over and introduced myself to Raquel's girlfriend.

TARYN: "It's nice to meet you, Wes."

I had no time for games, so I let my intentions be known right away.

ME: "Listen Taryn, I've had the longest day and I'm exhausted. However, I wanna hangout with you at another time. Why don't you take down my number and so we can hangout. Call me if you're interested. If not, then it was nice to meet you."
TARYN: "Sounds good. What are you doing after this?"
ME: "I'm on my way home."
TARYN: "Bummer. Raquel and I are staying at the Westin tonight and may have a get together if you'd like to come."
ME: "The Westin? I thought you two were from here?"

TARYN: "Yeah, but we have been drinking so we're going to take a cab to the hotel."

ME: "Alright. In any case, I'm headed home. If you do decide to have a get together then call me. You have my number."

I left JB with the two girls and headed back to my car. My place was a twenty-minute drive and I was delighted to finally get a chance to sleep in my own bed. Halfway through the drive, my phone started ringing from a number I didn't recognize. When I answered I recognized the voice. It was Taryn.

TARYN: "Wes, where are you? Have you made it home yet?"

ME: "I'm almost there."

TARYN: "Turn around; I want you to come over. We're staying at the Westin."

The average guy would have made a U-turn right after hearing these words. However, being the pussy-holic that I am, I made a V-turn.

Just as Taryn was giving me their room number JB called in on the other line.

JB: "Yo, you coming to the Westin?"

ME: "I'm on my way!"

JB: "I'll be there in five minutes. We about to show these girls what their pussy is made for! I've been trying' to fuck this bitch for weeks and it's finally about to go down. Matter of fact, I heard the one I got goes both ways. And we both know that birds of a feather..."

ME: "...will fuck each other even in the stormy weather!"

JB and I arrived at the Westin around the same time. We made it up to the room the girls were in. There were two queen beds that we had every intention of using. When JB entered the room he wasted no time. He wrapped his arms around Raquel and they began locking lips.

After Taryn greeted me she sat at the edge of the bed and started watching television. I made my way to the bed and sat next her. Next, Taryn rolled her eyes and sat on the floor next to my feet. I was baffled. I came all the way over here to have this woman calling out my name and she was now acting like she was pissed that I came up to the room.

Figuring that JB was suffering my current fate, I glanced over at his side of the room. Both JB and Raquel were still going at in the sheets. JB was under cover like the vice squad. His jeans were lying on the floor and his shirt was off. JB was about to have sex and in the game while I was just going to be a spectator on the sideline.

I played copycat and was hoping Taryn would follow my lead. I tossed my shirt and slid my jeans off then I got in the bed. I would have thought this would have caught Taryn's attention but she didn't even blink an eye. Her eyes were glued to the television.

I decided to count her as a loss and get some sleep. The sexual chemistry between Taryn and me was like a bad case of ADHD because it lacked any sort of attention. On the other side of the room, I could hear lips smacking, happy giggling and whole lot of whispering. If this were a race, JB was just about to cross the finish line and I hadn't even put my running shoes on.

Realizing that, at any moment, JB and Raquel were going to be bumpin' uglies, I tried to motivate Taryn. I got up from under the

covers, leaned over the edge of the bed where she was sitting and whispered in her ear.

> **ME:** "Why don't you come to bed? They are beating
> us! We have to do something. I'm over here looking like
> Boo-Boo the fool."
> **TARYN WASN'T IMPRESSED AT ALL.**
> **TARYN:** "I'll come to bed when I'm done watching TV.
> Thank you very much."

Taryn was being a bitch, but I was too tired to leave now and go home. I went back to my spot under the covers and closed my eyes to sleep. The harder I tried to sleep, the louder JB and Raquel were getting. I grew more and more frustrated.

I couldn't sleep, I couldn't pound between the sheets, I couldn't even get Taryn to taste my meat. I was envious of JB. He was getting all of the action. Obviously, Taryn wasn't interested in me. I decided to give it one more last chance. I whispered in Taryn's ear again.

> **ME:** "I know you said you wanted to watch the rest of the
> show but why don't you get off of the floor and come and
> watch it in bed with me."

Taryn didn't answer right away.

> **ME:** "Did you hear me?"

Taryn finally responded with a few words I had heard earlier that day from Katrina.

TARYN: "Yes, but I'm letting you know, now; I'm not having sex with you. I want to get that straight. "
ME: "That's fine. Who said we were sleeping together?"
TARYN: "Good cause I just met you. I don't know you enough to sleep with you."

Taryn changed in her pajamas and finally got into bed with me.

ME: "Goodnight."

I closed my eyes and tried to go to sleep once again. However, the fact that this tease had me drive all the way over to the Westin only to deny me of splitting her apple was driving me nuts.

ME: "Why did you have me come all the way over here tonight if you weren't trying to have sex?"
TARYN: "You think I'm just some girl you can fuck on the first night? I am a lady. I just wanted someone to hold. Can't a girl just have some company without worrying about a guy getting in her pants?"

Taryn was a lost cause. I felt like an American league pitcher during the World Series; I knew I wasn't going to hit. Therefore, I had to use some reverse psychology on her.

ME: "I was just asking. You know, sex isn't that important to me. I'm just happy to be here in bed with you. I'm hoping this will eventually evolve into something else."

Taryn was pleased with my statement because she started making out with me. While making out with her, I heard something jingling in the background. It was the sound of JB's belt. I looked up and JB was putting his clothes back on. Something was wrong and you could cut the tension in the room with a knife.

ME: "JB, you alright?"
HIS ENTIRE DEMEANOR HAD CHANGED FROM EARLIER.
JB: "Yeah, I'm about to leave."
ME: "Leave? We just got here."
JB: "You can stay. I'm leaving."

JB put on his clothes and left me in the room. That meant there were two beds, two girls and myself. I knew Taryn wasn't sleeping with me. I knew I was going to have a better chance with Raquel. JB had most likely got his girl hot and bothered and I figured I could help cool her off. I was there to satisfy needs.

RAQUEL: "Fuck this."

Raquel got out of the bed and started getting dressed.

TARYN: "Is everything OK?"
RAQUEL: "No! Fucking JB. I told him before he came here
that we weren't having sex. He kept trying anyway. All
guys are the same. They just want to fuck you."

Raquel was pissed and packing her bags. They say Hell has no fury like a woman scorned.

TARYN: "Are you leaving?"

RAQUEL: "Yes! I'm so ticked; I can't sleep here. I'm going home. Wes, when you see your friend, tell him he's an asshole!"

Feeling bad and uneasy about the whole situation. I interjected.

ME: "Just stay here. I will leave so that you and your girl can have the room to yourself."

Raquel wasn't trying to hear it. She and Taryn got into a mini verbal battle.

RAQUEL: "No, Wes, you can stay here. I'm leaving regardless."

Taryn: "So you are just leaving me here? I just paid good money for this room. You can't just leave me."

RAQUEL: "Goodnight, Wes, it was nice meeting you."

Raquel picked her bag up and shut the door behind her.

TARYN: "Wow! She just left me!"

The room was silent. No JB, no Raquel, just Taryn and me. Similar to a baseball player, I was working with two balls and Taryn had given me two strikes. Her words kept playing in the back of my mind. "I'm not having sex with you." She was like that house in the neighborhood that doesn't celebrate Halloween; she refused to

give up her candy. Instead of letting her words determine my fate, I swung for the fences and went into seduction mode.

> ME: "I know she just left you, but I'm right here with you, baby. I would never do that to you."

Taryn was eating it up.

> TARYN: "That means a lot to me. I'm glad you're here with me."

I flipped Taryn over and began rubbing her back. Within seconds, the woman started snoring.

> ME: "Taryn?"

I shook her a little bit.

> ME: "Taryn? Uh...are you awake?"
> TARYN: "Mmm hmm."

I flipped her back over.

> ME: "You're fading on me."

I began giving her a chest massage. She grabbed my hand and put it between her legs. I saw an ounce of daylight. I pulled her bottoms off.

> TARYN: "I think you're sexy as hell, but I don't want to regret this in the morning."

ME: "If you're going to regret this in the morning then we can sleep until the afternoon. I'm sure they have late check out."

TARYN: "OK, but what we do doesn't leave this room."

Taryn's bikini biscuit was now available like Father's day cards in the hood. We began having some of the best hotel sex. She turned over and bent over showing me her Marriott. I jumped in her Holiday Inn with my W. We went from being freezing to cool, to warm, and then to hot like the Four Seasons.

I guess it was feeling pretty good to her because she was using cusswords to describe the action.

TARYN: "Whoa shit! This fucking dick is fucking awesome."

She was being annoying, so I stuck out her head in the pillow.

TARYN: "%&$#?@!"

After shooting out my Ritz-Carlton, she finally removed herself from the pillow.

TARYN: "You are amazing! Oh shit. You just fucked the shit out of me."

Sunday

By now the sunlight was peeking through the curtains. Taryn was wide-awake and started packing her bags.

ME: "You're leaving as well?"

TARYN: "Yeah, you can sleep in. Check out isn't for another few hours. I'm going to catch a cab back to my car."

Out of the four people in a hotel room, I was the last man standing. A race is never won at the start, only at the finish line. It was like the tortoise and the hare. I thought JB was guaranteed to some Barracuda but in the end, I came out being the big fish. You just never know how a night can turn out.

I convinced Taryn to let me drop her at her car. Before I dropped her off there was one last question I had for her.

ME: "Your name is Taryn right?"

TARYN: "Yup. Call me sometime."

Although it was now broad daylight outside, I was falling asleep on my way home.

Once home, I crashed out on the couch for hours. That is, until a text message from Edna woke me up.

EDNA: "Are we still meeting up tonight?"

Edna was a girl I had met in passing a two weeks earlier shopping at the local grocery store. I had never hung out with her before but I had forgotten that we were supposed to meet at Panera Bread at 7pm.

The day had gone so fast and it was already 5:15 in the afternoon. I tried to rush to the gym to get a quick work out with JB. During the workout, I gave JB a play by play of the previous night.

JB: "I can't believe you fucked that bitch."

ME: "Me neither. I guess pussy comes to those who wait."

JB: "Yeah, I was way too impatient. But they both invited us to the hotel room at 3am. What did they think was going to go down? If they wanted to cuddle they should have bought teddy bears."

I looked up at the clock, it was now 6:45.

ME: "I have to cut this workout short. I have to meet this girl at Panera in fifteen minutes."

I left JB at the gym. He had been hitting the weights extremely hard, and I think he was still working out his sexual frustrations from the previous night. I was drenched in sweat but didn't have time to run home and shower. So, I changed clothes in the car and headed to Panera.

Edna was already in the restaurant.

ME: "Sorry, I'm running late."

EDNA: "It's cool. I just ordered a coffee without you. I hope you don't mind."

ME: "Not at all. Well the good news is that I'm here. Now what were your other two wishes?"

Edna laughed out loud.

EDNA: "So you're a comedian?"

ME: "I try but I'm not very good at it. Shall we have a seat?"

EDNA: "I think we shall."

Edna was a lot prettier than what I remembered. Another thing that I noticed was her larger-than-socially-acceptable breasts. Her love pillows were so big; my tongue was going to need to purchase airfare in order to get from one nipple to the other.

I began our conversation, asking about her interests and hobbies.

EDNA: "I really love to travel."
ME: "What is the most unique place you have been?"
EDNA: "One year, I got to go to Dubai for my job."
ME: "Really? Dubai? What was that like?"
EDNA: "It was so nice! Well, there was this one time when I went to a health spa to get a massage and it was really weird. They asked me to get down to nothing but a towel. Then all these women were trying to give me a bath. They kept staring at my breasts. They were infatuated with them. I guess they had never seen nothing like that. I asked them to stop but they kept insisting that they continue to wash me. I was uncomfortable at first but in the end it wasn't so bad."
ME: "I guess I'm going to have to make it to Dubai, so I can have women can wash me!"
EDNA: "I'm sure you would have no problems getting that done here."

Edna's comment opened up a whole can of worms. After that, we went into sex talk. We started talking about vibrators, funny sex stories, and previous relationships.

ME: "You were married before? What happened?"
EDNA: "Let's just say he had problems rising to the occasion."
ME: "You know they have things like Cialis and Viagra out there."
EDNA: "His pride got the best of him. So for two years, I was deprived of sex. Eventually our marriage fell apart."

With melons like you see in a watermelon patch, I knew I would have no problem rising to the occasion when the time was right.

We were so deep into conversation at Panera that they had closed and the employees were kicking us out.

EDNA: "Where should we go? You want to go grab something to drink?"
ME: "I wasn't expecting to have anyone over, but I have plenty of drinks at my place. Have you ever heard of the Purple Haze?"
EDNA: "What's that?"

I explained to Edna what a Purple Haze was. One thing my cousin Shawn always taught me was to have drinks at the house. One day he showed me how to make this drink called the Purple Haze. The recipe for the Purple Haze consists of Grape Vodka, Peach Schnapps, Blue Curacao, sweet and sour, Sprite, and Cranberry juice.

The purple haze tastes like a sweet tart and women love it. You can hardly taste the alcohol but before you know it, the Purple Haze will bring the freak out of anybody. That Purple Haze is the

type of drink that will have a sexual abstinent woman pregnant with twins. Before you know it, she will be naming one of her twins Rhee and the other one Grett.

> EDNA: "Yeah, I can come over. But before I do, I'm going
> to throw a disclaimer out there."

I got the feeling that Edna had a few famous words she had to tell me.

> ME: "I'm listening..."
> EDNA: "I am not sleeping with you. We are having a drink
> and nothing else. I want to make that clear."
> ME: "Who said anyone was sleeping with anyone? I wasn't
> even thinking like that. I was just thinking that we could
> sit on the couch and have a good time. To put that dis-
> claimer out there, the thought at least crossed your mind."
> EDNA: "Whatever. Just drive slowly so I can follow you to
> your place."

My place was not too far up the road. Once we got inside, Edna sat on my couch while I went to the kitchen to mix some drinks. I made myself a Jack and Coke but held the Jack. Next, I made Edna the infamous Purple Haze.

> EDNA: "Mmm. This drink is so good!"

We sat and watched the evening news, while she sipped on her drink.

> EDNA: "This drink kind of crept up on me! I am starting
> to feel it."

Thank you, Purple Haze.

EDNA: "I want another one of these drinks but I have to
drive home. I refuse to drink and drive."

I could tell my night was going to be ending soon. As soon as
Edna felt comfortable driving, she would be gone. There was one
problem. Like a family who didn't relocate, I hadn't made a move.
I figured I could at least get a kiss goodbye.
    I finally leaned over to kiss Edna.

EDNA: "What took you so long? I was wondering when
you were going to kiss me."

We started sucking face again and again....then, again once more.
This go around, Edna tried kissing me on my neck but I pulled
away. I was having a major issue. As much as I wanted to give her
a piece of my donut holder, I hadn't showered. This was a major
setback, like clocks during daylight savings.
    Edna stood up and grabbed her purse as if she was getting ready
to leave.

EDNA: "Thank you for a great night, Wes; I had so much
fun with you tonight. Call me tomorrow."

I wanted Edna so bad but I had too much pride to let her suck on any
part of my body after an intense gym workout without showering.
So, I had to get creative.

ME: "Can I ask you a question?"

EDNA: "Yes, What is it?"

ME: "Never mind, I don't think it's appropriate."

EDNA: "Well now you have to tell me, you already started..."

ME: "OK. I just want you to know; I think you are sexy as hell. Well, remember earlier at Panera, you were talking about Dubai?"

EDNA: "Yes."

ME: "Well ever since you mentioned how those women were giving you a bath, I couldn't help to think how hot that was. I have been wanting to do that with you."

EDNA: "I don't get it, what are you saying?"

ME: "I'm not saying anything is going to happen, but I really want you to take a shower with me. Right now. I can tell by our earlier conversations, you are a risk taker and love to be spontaneous. Here is your chance to show how spontaneous you can be."

Edna smiled, then thought for a minute.

EDNA: "I can't, because you know what that is going to lead to. I'm not going there on a first date."

ME: "So you're not a risk taker after all...Technically, it isn't our first date. This is our second date. Our first date was at Panera. It's ok to have a second date on the same day."

EDNA: "I guess you're right. You know what? Why not?"

It worked; I put some light jazz on and lit candles in the bathroom. I grabbed Edna's hand and walked her into the bathroom then turned the shower on. The steam from the shower increased and intensified the candlelight in the room, making it a perfect romantic scene.

Edna and I undressed each other and got underneath the water. We started grabbing for each other's tools like maintenance in the dark. I was washing her milk wagons; she was washing my meat and veggies. I was no longer sweaty and ready to jump in her briar patch.

ME: "I want to have sex so bad."
EDNA: "No we can't remember? I said we aren't doing that."

Before I could respond to Edna, she quickly had a change of heart.

EDNA: "Wait a second, do you have a condom?"
ME: "Yup! They're in the other room."
EDNA: "OK, let's do it."
ME: "Stay right here."

I ran out of the shower, grabbed a condom, and was back in the shower in no time. With the water still running in the shower, we started having liquid sex. We then moved from the shower to the bathroom counter, then to the bedroom.

Edna and I had sex about three times that night. So much so that we didn't stop until 4:00 am. Edna was very intent on not sleeping with me originally. It was shocking how the night turned out. It was like a woman leaving an abandoned kitten on my front porch; I was surprised she gave me the pussy.

Monday

It was now Monday afternoon and my sperm shooter had been busting shots for the past few days. I was back at my place talking to my brother Will on the phone.

ME: "You will never guess what has happened to me the past few days..."

I explained all the events that had taken place since the following Thursday. I told him how every woman made it a point to tell me that they weren't sleeping with me, and then...*voila!* They are perched on my pickle.

Will: "You're on fire! Sometimes it gets like that. You have to take advantage when you can. When you're hot, you're hot."

As I was talking to Will, a text message came in from Pia.

PIA: *Hey handsome. When are we going to finally hangout?*

I gave Will a play-by-play.

ME: "This girl, Pia, is texting me right now."
WILL: "What is she saying?"
ME: "She is asking me when she and I are going to hangout."
WILL: "You might as well go hang with her tonight."

Since it was a Monday, I had no plans.
    I sent a text to Pia.

ME: *Let's hangout tonight. I'll come over there, and maybe we can watch a movie.*

Pia wasn't a very attractive woman. If I had a quarter for every time I saw a woman as ugly as Pia, I would have twenty-five cents. Pia was a girl that approached me and got my number before I flew out

of town to Charlotte. I only gave her my number because I figured she was a girl that I could practice all my lines on.

Pia responded right away.

PIA: *You can come over but don't expect anything to happen. I hope you don't think you are coming here just to have sex.*
ME: *I'm not.*
PIA: *OK, I'm just making sure.*

I relayed her message to Will on the phone.

WILL: "There you go! *Famous last words.* You better hurry up and head over there."
ME: "She isn't all that though."
WILL: "What else do you have to lose? I'm getting off the phone. You have business to attend to."

Will hung up the phone.

Pia was a *glad to be there* woman. These are the women that are just glad to be in your presence. They are just happy to be there when you call them or go over to their place. Typically, these types of women are at least a five or lower on a scale of ten.

They are like the twelfth man on an NBA roster. Technically they are on the team but you wouldn't dare give them any playing time. You want them to stay in their warm up sweats on the bench. Mondays are reserved for the *glad to be there* woman. Nothing exciting really goes on during a Monday and it is one of the few days of the week where you can afford to hang out with them.

Pia sent me her address via text. She had just moved back to Pittsburgh from San Diego and was staying at her father's house. Her father worked the graveyard shift, so he left every night around 10:30 pm.

PIA: "When you get here, don't ring the doorbell. Just call me so I can sneak you in the basement."

When I arrived, Pia was glad I even showed up. She smuggled me down to the basement like an illegal immigrant.

PIA: "What do you want to watch?"

We settled on watching *American Horror Story*. Being next to her, I felt like I was living a real life horror story. Twenty minutes into the show I heard a male voice yell from up the stairs.

MALE VOICE: "Pia, I'm leaving. I'll see you tomorrow."
PIA: "Have a goodnight at work. Love you, Dad."

We were now home alone like Macaulay Culkin. While the television show was running, my mind was racing. I was contemplating making a move. Then I thought what Will had said earlier. "Take advantage when you can."

I looked over at Pia. I looked down at Mr. Dickie. Back at Pia. Then back to Mr. Dickie. In my mind, I gave him some encouragement.

ME: "I hope you're ready Mr. Dickie. I'm going to need you to perform like the phallus I raised you to be. Give it your all!"

Like jumping into swimming pool, I closed my eyes and held my breath. I leaned over to Pia and started giving her a tonsil swab. We began swapping spit till the television show went off. In between giving her a tonsilectomy, I was giving her free breast exams.

PIA: "Damn you're sexy. I'm just glad that you're over here. At first I thought you might not show up."

There you have it folks. Even Pia knew she was a *glad to be there* woman. Since I had made it second base already, I decided to bring it on home.

ME: "I'm so glad, I showed up. You are so sexy."
PIA: "Really? Nobody has ever told me that before."

Yeah, that's because I was the only guy dumb enough to lie to your ass. When I told Pia she was sexy, it drove her over the top.

PIA: "I want you so bad, but I'm afraid of what you might think of me. I want to hang out with you but you always seemed busy in the past. Since this is our first time actually chilling together, I want you to call me tomorrow. What days are you usually free?"
ME: "Mondays. Well, actually...some Mondays. Any other day I'm busy. I tend to work a lot."
PIA: "Maybe we can hangout next Monday."
ME: "I'm sure we might be able to work something out. And going back to your earlier statement, I would never, ever think of you any less if we had sex."

I said the magic words. Pia pulled her clothes off so fast, you would have thought they were on fire.

In my head I gave Mr. Dickie more motivation.

ME: "Mr. Dickie, now it's your time! Get in there and show her what you're made of! Vein for vein, inch for inch, show her why you should be shaft of the year!"

Pia grabbed Mr. Dickie and put him inside. I started giving it to her on the couch. I could hear a cheer in the back of my head, which sounded like it was coming from Mr. Dickie.

MR. DICKIE: "U-G-L-Y, you ain't got no alibi...you ugly. M-A-M-A, how you think you got that way? Yo' momma, yo momma."

I had her father's couch rockin'. It felt like I was rearranging furniture down there. I was proud of Mr. Dickie for his efforts. After we finished, I left like a thief in the night. Currently, Pia is still waiting on that Monday to hangout. I haven't hung out with her again. But when I do, she will be glad...to be there.

Famous last words are defined as a notable final utterance before the death of an individual. In a span of a few days, "I'm not sleeping with you" was a phrase spoken by many. Edna, Kathy, Katrina, Edna and Taryn all had one thing in common. *Famous last words.*

Chapter 21

The Encore

One day, I gave an unforgettable encore performance.

I was in Tampa for two weeks with my coworkers at a work convention. It was summer time and there were plenty of people on vacation. While checking into the hotel, my co-workers spotted two hot women walking through the lobby. My co-worker Billy was one of the first to notice them.

> **BILLY:** "Wes, you see those two over there?"
> **ME:** "Where?"
> **BILLY:** "Uh, seven o'clock."

When I turned, it was already too late. A few of my other co-workers were already talking to them. Fine women are like a fumble in a football game; everyone scrambles to get it but usually only one person comes up with it. Unlike the Colts, my coworkers were like the rest of the thirty-one teams in 2012 NFL draft, they came up with no Luck.

> **ME:** "What happened?"
> **RYAN:** "They are stuck up. They wanted no part of us."

ME: "Did you get their names at least?"
RYAN: "Yeah, Janelle and Heather. They said they just got in from New Orleans. I guess they go to Tulane University."

For those of you that are not familiar with Tulane...let's just say when you take a party school and place it in the city of New Orleans, you have a year round Mardi Gras. Janelle and Heather would go to the pool every day at the same time to tan. Throughout the week, guys would try to hit on them but only get denied.

They were good eye candy for all of us, however, we could look but were far from touching. Then one evening all of that changed.

We all decided to go out to the Coyote Ugly Saloon in Ybor City. We piled up in three separate cabs and headed down there. When we arrived to *Coyote Ugly*, the bartenders were dancing on top of the tables. It was just like you see in the movies: sexy women in cowboy boots serving drinks. Being in Coyote Ugly must have raised a few of my coworkers' testosterone levels because they were ready to head to the strip club.

RYAN: "Let's head over to Skin! I've heard the strippers over there are all perfect tens!"

Although there was a big group of us, I wasn't in the mood to go to a strip club. I didn't feel like giving random stranger money so they could give me the tease of a lifetime.

ME: "I'm going to head back to the hotel."

I left my coworkers and caught a cab back to the hotel. Instead of going straight to my room, I stopped by the bar to watch some television. There were maybe three men at the bar. It was empty like a one hit wonder's concert. We were all pathetic and lonely.

BARTENDER: "What can I get for you?"
ME: "Just some water, I'm trying to watch the tail end of this baseball game."

While watching the game, I heard a woman's voice behind me.

WOMAN'S VOICE: "Cosmo please."

When I looked up, it was Janelle. She was wearing a pair of 7 jeans and had a caboose. I'm like an old school farmer, I love my asses big.

JANELLE: "Hi, is this seat taken?"
ME: "Not at all. Have a seat."
JANELLE PULLED UP TO THE SEAT NEXT TO ME.
JANELLE: "Hi, I'm Janelle. What's your name?"
ME: "Yeah, I saw you when I checked in. I'm Wes."
JANELLE: "What are you doing alone at the bar? You waiting on someone?"
ME: "I'm just watching this baseball game. I'm not waiting on anyone, just here by myself."
JANELLE: "The night is still young. What are you doing here by yourself? There is a whole city out there."
ME: "I went out with a few friends but I decided to retire early."

Janelle and I stayed at the bar getting to know each other. I noticed that she had burn marks all over her left arm.

> **ME:** "If you don't mind me asking, what happened to your arm?"

Janelle: "I was at a bar in New Orleans and I ordered a flaming shot. To make a long story short, when I went to drink the shot, somehow the alcohol spilled on my arm and the whole side of my arm went up in flames. I sued the bar and got a huge settlement. That's the reason why I'm out here on vacation to get away from everything. I needed a change in scenery."

Janelle took a few sips from her drink. I noticed throughout our conversation she was showing indicators that she was interested in me. The more I leaned away from her, the more she leaned in forward. Well into the conversation, I felt like she would bite my bait so I threw it out there.

> **ME:** "I'm headed back to my room to relax and see what's on TV. If you're not doing anything, come up."
> **JANELLE:** "Well, my friend Heather wants me to go back to our room and meet this guy she recently met…"
> **ME:** "…okay"
> **JANELLE:** "But after that I will come visit you. What room are you in?"
> **ME:** "243."

I gave a Janelle a quick hug and headed for my room. While en route to my room, I became aware that many of my coworkers had

made it back from being out. A lot of them continued partying in the room next to mine.

RYAN: "We're having a Madden tournament. You want in? We're placing fifty dollar bets. Come strong or don't come at all."
ME: "I'm good. I'm headed back to the room. I'll see you in the morning."

I walked in my room hopped in the shower, and like a grocery store employee, I quickly washed my fruit. It wasn't too long before I heard a soft knock at the door. Since peepholes tend to make everything larger than life, I noticed two gigantic mammaries staring back at me. I opened the door and addressed each mammary by name.

I turned toward the left.

ME: "Hello Ma'am."

I turned to the right.

ME: "Hello Ma'am."

Janelle was looking at me like I was crazy.

JANELLE: "You're too funny. Why do you keep calling me ma'am? That makes me feel old."
ME: "I figured since you're from the south, I would pay homage."
JANELLE: "Thank you, sir."

Janelle came in and sat at the edge of my bed. We could hear the cheers and sudden bursts of celebrations next door.

> **JANELLE:** "Wow, it's loud over there. They must be having a party."
> **ME:** "Those are just my coworkers. They are having a video game tournament. Those things can get intense."

We began watching the television show Criminal Minds in order to drown out the sound coming from the ruckus next door. While watching the show, I leaned over to kiss Janelle. We fondled each other for a few minutes. Next, I heard a loud knock coming from outside.

> **JANELLE:** "Are you expecting someone?"
> **ME:** "Not that I know of."

I got up to check the peephole. There was nobody there. I opened the door to see who was knocking. It was a false alarm. The knock we heard was hotel security, asking my coworkers to keep the noise level down.

Janelle and I got back to business. She must have been an astronomer because she couldn't wait to see my big dipper. She whipped my hoe-handle out and kissed it like she missed it.

Judging by her intelligence, she was far from being Tulane's Valedictorian. But she was a *valid dictorian*. It was obvious that she was the authority when it came to studying dick.

Additionally, I could have referred to her as electricity because she gave head at the speed of light. After a messy bed, a wet

pecker, and two used condoms on the floor, I sent Janelle on her way.

I sat next to Billy and Ryan the next morning at breakfast.

BILLY: "How was your night last night?"

ME: "It was fantastic."

RYAN: "Yeah we heard all about it! Just food for thought, though, when you decide to watch porn in the hotel, at least turn the volume down a bit."

ME: "Porn? What porn?"

BILLY: "Yeah, we heard your TV from the other room."

ME: "That was no TV. That was all me."

RYAN: "Well, you sound like a bitch. So you're trying to tell us that when we saw you leaving the bars last night… alone…you magically had a girl come to your room? I wonder how much that hooker cost you."

ME: "Free, ninety nine. You guys remember those girls from New Orleans? Well, that was Janelle surround sounding off in my room last night."

BILLY: "You mean those girls from Tulane?"

ME: "Yeah."

BILLY: "I meant to tell you, I ran into Heather the other day and she was telling me…"

Ryan quickly cut Billy off.

RYAN: "…I'm gonna call you out and flat out tell you. You're lying on your dick. There is no way you had sex with her. Everyone in the lobby was trying to hit that. So

now you're telling me you, of all people, fucked her last night and nobody was there to witness it? Get outta here. I'm not believing it. I'm calling bullshit on this one."
Billy nodded his head in agreement.

ME: "You don't believe me?"
RYAN: "Hell no. There was no way that was her. Now if you would have told me you had some fat ugly bitch in the room I might have believed you. But her...no way. You were watching porn last night; you're just too embarrassed to admit it."
ME: "There's no way for me to prove it."
RYAN: "If you ever get to hook up with her, take a pic of her and show it to us.   It'll prove you hooked up with her."
BILLY: "Matter of fact, just take a regular pic of her in your room. I don't even believe she has seen the inside of your hotel room."

The audience was demanding proof of Janelle, which I was determined to give them.

ME: "I have one even better."
RYAN: "What? The only thing better is a hidden camera in the room."
ME: "Nope. How about an encore?"
RYAN: "An encore?"
ME: "Yeah an encore. A repeat performance of what I did last night. Only this time, you and whoever else can watch me, live."

Ryan and Billy leaned in as if they couldn't believe what I was saying.

> **BILLY:** "How are you going to pull that off?"
> **RYAN:** "Are we gonna hide in one of your room closets?"
> **ME:** "Easy. I'll invite her over tonight. When she comes to my room, I just won't close the curtains all the way. And I will leave the lights on."
> **BILLY:** "That'll work."
> **RYAN:** "I'll be anxious to see what this encore is all about."

That afternoon I arranged with Janelle to come to my room around eight that evening. Everyone who saw Janelle thought she was sexy as hell. Janelle was like a bass drum on display at a music store; every time you walked passed her, you wanted to beat.

Meanwhile, I arranged with Ryan to give him a signal to come out and look through the window. I was to pick up the phone, dial his room and pretend like I was calling the hotel operator for a wakeup call.

Later that night, when the clock got closer to eight, I began to get nervous. Not nervous about Janelle but nervous about performing before my peers. Our peers are the hardest critics and I had to give them the show of their lifetimes.

As I waited in my room, I pulled my pants away from my waistline, looked down and gave my pecker a pep talk. One that was familiar. The good ol' Al Pacino, *Any Given Sunday* speech.

> **ME:** "I don't know what to say, really. Three minutes to the biggest battle of our sex lives. It all comes down to

tonight, and either we do this as a team, or we're gonna crumble.   Inch by inch, position by position."

I continued my pathetic rant in order to make sure he understood the magnitude of this lay.

ME: "You find out sex is this game of inches, so is football. Because in either game—sex or football—the margin for error is so small. I mean, one half a step too late or too early and you don't quite make the cut. One half second too slow, too fast and she doesn't reach orgasm."

I quickly wrapped up my speech.

ME: "The inches we need during sex are everywhere around us. They're in every break of the game, every minute, every second. In this room we will fight for that inch. On this team we tear ourselves and everyone else around us to pieces for that inch. She will claw with her fingernails for that inch. Because we know when we add up all those inches, that's gonna make the fucking difference between winning and losing! Between making love and flat out bangin!"

By now, my pecker was like a fish out of water; he couldn't wait to get wet. I prepped the room so that the curtains were open enough so people could see in without making it too obvious.

Janelle arrived to my room a little after 8:30. Although she had a nice mini skirt on and was dressed like a woman of the night, she looked a little loopy.

ME: "You're already drunk? It's only eight."

Janelle came over and started kissing me right away.

> **JANELLE:** "Baby, baby, baby. I'm not drrrrunk. I'm just a
> little itsy bitsy tipsy."
> **ME:** "How much have you had to drink?"

Janelle didn't answer. She just sat in the chair looked up at the ceiling and began blowing spit bubbles.

Even though she was acting a little strange, the audience demanded an encore, which they were not going to get if she didn't sober up.

She stood up and gave me a big hug. Then, she grabbed my pee-pee.

> **JANELLE:** "I so missed you today. I need you to give me
> some of this right now."

Since time was ticking, I gave Janelle instructions.

> **ME:** "I have to get up early tomorrow. So why don't you
> get naked while I call to the front for a wakeup call?"

Janelle began getting naked without any hesitation. I picked up the phone and dialed room 241.

> **RYAN:** "Is she in there?"
> **ME:** "Yes. Can I please get a wakeup call for seven o'clock?"

Janelle began kissing me on the back of my neck.

RYAN: "Make sure you leave the lights on so we can see!"
ME: "Okay, so that is confirmed."
RYAN: "We are going to head next door in about two minutes. You better already be in the pussy by the time we get there."
ME: "Thank you."

It was now game time. I was determined to put on the performance of a lifetime. I was about to be under lights. I positioned Janelle face down on the bed but facing the window to let the audience watch.

JANELLE: "Oh, yeah, Daddy; give it to me!"

Janelle started moaning like a porn star once again. Hearing sexual sounds for the second night in a row triggered the perverts to come to the window. It was now time to give them a show. I could barely see through the crack in the curtains but I knew they could see me in Janelle's end zone. Since they were peering through, I provided them with a few shout outs.

I pointed at the window using my index finger while simultaneously pumping Janelle's snatch. One pump, two pump, I threw up two index fingers giving them the peace sign. Three pump, four pump, five pump, five and a half pump; I threw up a double peace sign.

Six pump, seven pump, I pretended like I had an Uzi and sprayed them all with my invisible bullets. Eight pump, nine pump, ten pump, eleven pump; I raised both hands in the air and raised

the roof. Then raised the roof again. I grabbed her hips and went Speedy Gonzales on that ass. By the twenty ninth pump, I raised my left hand to my mouth and acted as if I was yawning.

I was showboating in the pussy, which was going to make an unforgettable encore. Next, I placed my hands behind my head and interlocked my fingers as if I was under arrest.

Since I was thrusting so hard, Janelle fell forward and was no longer on her hands and knees. She was now flat or her stomach. This only made me go faster. By now I was looking like a Chihuahua on crack. I started making faces by crossing my eyes. I just knew Billy and Ryan were on the other side of the window laughing their ass off.

I started slapping Janelle's ass.

ME: "You like that?"

Janelle didn't respond.

I slapped her ass even harder.

ME: "You like that?"

Again, Janelle didn't respond. Then I became aware of an important detail. Janelle wasn't screaming like she had before. I pulled out. Janelle was on her stomach, motionless. I shook her.

ME: "Janelle? You okay?"

I listened to hear if she was breathing. Janelle was out.

ME: "Janelle?"

Janelle wasn't responding. I began to panic. I literally started to hyperventilate. I heard the door shut next door. Ryan and Billy had gone back in their room. I threw on my pants and ran next door.

ME: "I think Janelle is dead!"
BILLY: "Did you check her pulse?"
ME: "No but she isn't responding to anything."
RYAN: "At least she went out with a bang!"
ME: "Do I call 911?"

I rushed back to my room. Janelle hadn't moved. I reached over with two fingers and checked her pulse. Lub-dub-lub-dub-lub-dub.

ME: "She's alive!"

I shook her again.

I ran to the bathroom and threw a towel over her naked body. I didn't want to call 911. What was I going to tell them? This was a potential crime scene and there were at least two witnesses. I ran back to room 241.

BILLY: "I'll call her Heather! What room are they in?"
ME: "115."

Billy dialed 115.

BILLY: "Hi, Heather; its Billy from upstairs. Remember me? Well there is a certain situation going on with your friend

Janelle right now…I don't know how to say this but she is not responding. Does she have any health problems? I think we need to call 911. She was hanging out with Wes and just passed out. She has a pulse but is motionless."

Billy began listening intensely.

BILLY: "Uh huh…I see. Are you shittin' me? Oh yeah, that's right!"
ME: "What? What is she saying?"

Billy ignored my inquiries and continued talking to Heather.

BILLY: "OK, I'll let him know."

Billy hung up the phone.

RYAN: "What did she say?"
BILLY: "If you call 911, you're fucked. This is what I was trying to tell you the other day about this crazy broad. It just slipped my mind. Well anyway, Heather told me this girl does this all the time. Since she came into all this money she parties hard. When Janelle goes out, she takes GHB."
ME: "GHB? What is GHB?"
BILLY: "GHB is also known as the date rape drug. That girl is fucked up and unconscious in your room. Heather said she took it right before coming to see you tonight."
RYAN: "That's deep!"

ME: "Let me get this straight. Let's back up! You mean to tell me this crazy bitch came to my room wanting to have sex with me while on GHB?"
BILLY: "Yup."
RYAN: "And guess what? You call 911 and now you're going to jail for drugging an innocent girl you met at the bar in the hotel room. She will never admit to taking that on her own accord."
BILLY: "Heather said just give her some time and it will wear off."
ME: "How long will that take?"
BILLY: "According to Heather, at least six hours."

I left Billy and Ryan and went back to my room.

The situation couldn't have been any better for me to go to jail. I had a naked unconscious bombshell in my room with the date rape drug in her system. To make matters worse, I hadn't even known this girl that long. The only thing I knew about her was that she went to Tulane, she was on vacation with her girlfriend and she gave blowjobs like she was in fast forward.

I stayed up that night watching Janelle's ass stuck up in the air. When the morning came, Janelle finally woke up and showed some signs of life.

JANELLE: "What time is it? I have the biggest headache."

Janelle popped up like nothing happened and began getting dressed.

JANELLE: "I hope I wasn't too wild last night. I think I had a little too much to drink. I blacked out."

I didn't dare mention anything that happened the previous night. Janelle finished getting dressed and walked out of my room.

JANELLE: "Call me later; I think I'm going to go to the mall. Let me know if you want to come shopping with us."

Once Janelle left, I realized that I was with a woman that was wilder than I was. Another day hanging out with Janelle was going to get me in trouble.   I never met a girl that got off on slipping herself a Mickey. This is what happens when you give in to the demands of the audience.   Needless to say, Ryan and Billy experienced the ultimate encore.

Chapter 22

The Cookie Monster Phase

Cookie monster from Sesame Street is unable to stop once he starts eating; he can't control his appetite. Enter the cookie monster phase. A phase in life that almost everyone goes through when all you want is cookie.

Sometimes the Cookie Monster phase happens gradually. Other times it hits you on the head when you least expect it like a bad blowjob. Either way, once you have entered the cookie monster phase, it's impossible to think straight. All you can think about is cookie.

Cookie is known for making grown men go broke, cry, beg, fall in love and do things they normally would not do. Cookie has many different names such as the vagina, cunt, the peacekeeper, moneybox, kitty cat, lady's welcome mat, and many others.

It just so happened that one summer I entered the cookie monster phase after a significantly long cookie drought. I deprived myself of cookie in order to focus on myself. I stopped cold turkey. I was no longer attempting to pick up on women and the ones I had, I decided to cut off.

No more cookies for me. This type of mindset lasted for a long time, I would say for about a week.

Then one day I was in the mall and ran into a fortune cookie wearing workout clothes.

She was headed northbound; I was headed southbound. She seemed to be preoccupied and in deep conversation on the phone. Little did she know, I was about to be a part of her fortune.

ME: "Excuse me..."

She told whoever was on the other line to hold.

JENNIFER: "Yes?"

I pointed down at her feet,

ME: "Your shoe is untied."
JENNIFER: "Why, thank you."

She ditched whoever was on the other line.

JENNIFER: "Can you hold this bag for me while I tie my shoe?"

After some small talk, I found out we happened to both be members of the same gym. We then went our separate ways because I was still trying my best to avoid cookie. It seemed as though the more I tried to stay away from cookie, the more it was being thrown my way. All kinds of vanilla wafers, sugar cookies, some chips, were hitting me on ahoy and who can forget about the chocolate chunks.

I now noticed Jennifer every time I she was in my gym. As fine as she was, I only saw her as a friend. We would frequently talk about healthy foods and different types of exercises. Then one day the inevitable happened to me. While I was in between a set, Jennifer made an offer I wanted to reject.

JENNIFER: "I am making some stir fry tonight; you are more than welcome to come join me."

Somehow my words left my mouth like a C-section; the words were planned to come out one way but instead got delivered another way.

ME: "Sure, I'll be over there at eight."

When I arrived at Jennifer's house, I walked through the door with the intentions to maintain my strong willpower. However, after seeing Jennifer's tight jeans, knee high boots, and her hair done, my willpower quickly became *Wespower*.

She offered me a seat on her couch and I intentionally sat at the opposite side of the couch from her.

She gave me a disgusted look.

JENNIFER: "Can I ask you a question?"
ME: "You got it."
JENNIFER: "Are you not attracted to me? 'Cause most guys are constantly hitting on me. But with you...you just seem so uninterested, so uninvolved."
ME: "No, it's not that, I'm just talking a break from women right now."

JENNIFER: "A break from women?"

ME: "I'm just trying to focus on me right now. No booty calls, no dates, no girlfriends; nothing."

Jennifer saw my comment as a challenge. She charged me like MasterCard and began seducing me. She got up and straddled me then locked her lips on to mine. She began moving her tongue around in my mouth as if she was trying to dial the combination to my throat.

She began breathing heavy, like Darth Vader experiencing an asthma attack. I could no longer resist her advances and I started ripping the fortune cookie out of its packaging. As soon as I stuck my rolling pin in her uncharted waters I experienced the side effects of good cookie: my vision went blurry, my eyes crossed and I started breathing like a graduated in the top 10% from Lamaze class. I went from 20/20 vision to 20/300 vision in a matter of milliseconds. I could only repeat in my head what Cookie Monster says every day. ME LIKE COOKIE!

After opening Jennifer's box, I opened Pandora's box and entered what I call the Cookie Monster Phase. I was just like the Cookie Monster. *Me want more cookie and more and more and more.* After Jennifer's house, cookie started coming out of the woodwork.

First, there was Lynette she was like a Circus animal cookie because she was always trying to put her pink camel in my mouth. Secondly, there was a red head named Ashley. She was only 4'11 and I considered her my strawberry shortcake. Next was Natasha who loved to snicker and begged for me to doodle inside of her.

Then there was Maggie who was my Macadamian, she always begged for my nut. After Maggie, I met an Oreo named Holly. Co-

incidentally, she was half black and half white but I referred to her as Oreo, because she once told me that she liked to be double stuffed.

During my short time in the cookie monster phase, I had a variety of cookies ranging from Lemon cookies to Gingerbreads and from Peanut butter to Oatmeal Raisin.

I was being so reckless during this cookie monster phase, I finally had to stop because I slept with two girls who my friends had recently broken up with.

Rosa was an Italian Biscotti and well put together. She had the looks, the personality and the body.   She was the type of girl that grown men would put on their Christmas list. Rosa was like the sun coming up on an old country farm; she could make all the cocks rise.

Rosa seemed like the perfect girl that anyone would want to wife up. However, she had a jealous ex-boyfriend, Brody. Brody looked like a wrestler from the WWE because he was 6'3" and 275 pounds of pure muscle. For the most part, Brody was a nice gentleman outside of his relationship with Rosa.

When Rosa and Brody were an item, he would threaten to beat up anyone who remotely stared at his girl. Brody was a control freak. I never believed it until one day a few eyewitnesses saw Brody throw a punch and clock another man in the face for trying to talk to Rosa. That is what finally led to Rosa breaking it off with Brody. He loved that girl to death.   Brody was like a carne asada burrito; he was all wrapped up.

To complicate matters, Brody was one of my acquaintances and would confide in me with certain matters.

BRODY: "I don't understand why Rosa just left me stranded. Our relationship was so perfect."

ME: "You guys were together for a while. Sometimes relationships just grow sour for whatever reason. She could have thought you weren't the one or she could have found someone else. We will never know."

BRODY: "If I ever find out she is talking to another guy, I'm going to kill him."

ME: "But you two are broken up. Who cares what she does?"

BRODY: "I do. I'd rather be put in prison than be without her."

Brody was starting to sound like a mad man. The sad thing was, I knew he wasn't playing. I felt bad for the next person that gets with Rosa because there was about to be a target on his chest.

A few weeks after Brody's conversation, my doorbell rang. It was Ximara holding a big pot of spaghetti.

Ximara was dating my friend Nick.

XIMARA: "Hey, Wes, is Nick here?"

ME: "Yes, he is in the back. What are you bringing us?"

XIMARA: "We are bringing you dinner tonight."

ME: "We? What do you mean; we?"

XIMARA: "Oh, I brought Rosa with me. She is back at the car getting the rest of the stuff. We made you guys dinner. I hope you don't mind."

I paused for a second while my life flashed before my eyes.

ME: "Do you want me to die?"

Rosa started walking up to the door.

> **XIMARA:** "Great, I'm glad you're excited to eat with Rosa.
> We'll get started on the plates."

Ximara made her way through the door and Rosa followed suit.

I could already tell that the situation was not going to end well. I
was in the cookie monster phase. Rosa and Ximara came to prepare
a surprise dinner for my roommate and me. That idea was as good
as Conrad Murray administering drugs to Michael Jackson. If Brody
were to stop by, we would all be dead.

While the women were preparing the food in the kitchen, I
tried to prevent myself from thinking nasty thoughts about Rosa.
It was one of the hardest things I have had to do. I began thinking about Rosa's Italian Biscotti and how I wanted to treat it like
cookie batter. I wanted to whip it, beat it, and heat it up.

As we sat down to eat dinner, I stayed to myself while Nick,
Ximara, and Rosa were all talkative. Rosa caught wind of it.

> **ROSA:** "Why are you so quiet tonight?"
> **ME:** "Well, for two reasons. One, I am trying to hurry
> up and eat because I am supposed to go a house party
> tonight. Two, I know you and Brody just broke up and I
> have to get used to not seeing you two together."
> **ROSA:** "They key word is BROKE UP. We broke up and
> who knows what he is doing now. I'm sure he is fucking
> some other bitch. But it doesn't matter. We aren't
> together."

I began convincing myself that Rosa was right. After dinner, Nick and Ximira left to go to Nick's room. This left me sitting at the table with a finished plate of spaghetti and sitting across from me, cookie.

ROSA: "I have never seen your room. You want to show it to me?"
ME: "M-my room?"
ROSA: "Yeah, you know the place where you sleep."

I lead Rosa to my room and began showing her around.

ME: "This is my bed, my bathroom, and my closet."

Rosa pointed behind me towards the floor.

ROSA: "Those are some cool shoes what are those?"

As my attention got diverted towards the shoes, Rosa grabbed my shoulders. She turned me toward her and started kissing me. Being already in the cookie monster phase, I didn't even try to fight it. We moved over to the bed and caressed each other's bodies. I completely forgot about Brody and focused on the cookie. I began to think like the Cookie Monster: *C is for cookie and cookie is for me!* I even started to reason like the Cookie Monster: *Sometimes me think what is love. And then me think love is what last cookie is for. Yep, her give up the last cookie for me. Matter of fact, her give up all the cookies for me.*

Before I knew it, her bra and panties were off and I began playing with her Jammie Dodger. Next, Rosa started to put in a bid.

Rosa: "I want you to eat my pussy."

I hesitated.

I looked up at Rosa. Then, back to the pussy. Back to Rosa. Again, back at the pussy.

Me: "Um..."
Rosa: "What are you waiting for? I want you right here, right now."

After hearing those last seven words, I ate the pussy like four plus four. *Me WANT cookie! Me EAT cookie! Omm-nom-nom-nom-nom!*

I ate her Galbaldi Biscuit like it was the last meal on Earth. My cookie monster mindset continued. *Me not exactly TAKE the Cookie; me EAT the cookie!* All of the cookie eating eventually led me to smashing the cookie.

Her cookie was a little too good, because after a few minutes, I was shooting out my Chips Ahoy.

Rosa: "I want it all over me!"

It appeared that Rosa loved frosting on top of her cookie. Thereafter, she got what she asked for. Cookie and cream.

When we walked back out to the living room, Ximara and Nick were sitting on the sofa. I had cookie crumbs all over my face and Rosa looked like the Gingerbread man just nailed her.

Ximara: "Well hello there! I see that some of us have started the night off right. Rosa, you ready to get out of here?"

Nick gave me the "what in the hell were you thinking" look.

I walked the girls out to their car and Rosa gave me her number. I jumped in the car on the way to the house party. When I arrived to the party, people had been drinking for a while and were lit like a Christmas tree. When I walked in, I recognized one of my running mates, Rico. He was slurring his words like Daffy Duck.

RICO: "Wes! Where you been all night? Grab a beer!"
ME: "I'm good, just came over to say 'hello'. How is everything with you?"
RICO: "Shit sucks. You remember Danae?"
ME: "Yeah, your girlfriend?"
RICO: "My ex-girlfriend. She dumped me not too long ago."
ME: "You got caught cheating didn't you?"
RICO: "No I should have cheated on the bitch. My dumb ass was faithful. Anyway, she sends a text message the other day and says she wants to date other people. Other people? Can you believe that shit?"

Rico was all bent out of shape over this girl.

RICO: "Then she had the audacity to break up over a text message."
RICO: "And get this…She is here tonight. Just so happened she came to the same party I'm at."
ME: "Just be cordial and say hello."
RICO: "I'm not saying shit to her. Well, whatever, I'm on my way out. I hope some guy takes that slut home and fucks the shit out of her. She's a dumb bitch."

Rico had a grudge, like Sarah Michelle Gellar. He left the party drunk, depressed and discombobulated. I continued on inside the house saying hello to a few friends. I heard whooping and hollering coming from the kitchen by the belligerent partygoers. As I made my way toward the kitchen, the chants grew louder.

CROWD: "Shot! Shot! Shot! Shot!"

I turned the corner and saw Danae lying on the kitchen counter while a random guy was doing a body shot off of her.

A body shot is such a sexual way of doing tequila shots. The crowd erupted louder into a cheer. The guy grabbed her hand so that she could sit up. A nicely boozed up Danae looked over at me.

DANAE: "Wes! I fucking love you! Get your ass over here I need to take a shot!"
ME: "I'm going to pass. You're not gonna have me on that counter."
DANAE: "Not a body shot. A blow job…shot."

Danae was trying to get screwed like a Phillips head.

ME: "What's that?"

Danae grabbed another shot glass full of Tequila. The party goers started to chant again while banging their fists on the counter.

CROWD: "Blooow-job, bloooow-job, bloooow-job!"

Danae walked towards me enough to invade my personal space. She acted as if she was going to kiss me. Just before her lips pressed

me she reached down and grabbed my crotch. Next, she leaned over and whispered in my ear.

DANAE: "Watch and enjoy."

Danae got down on both knees. She unzipped my fly and placed her shot glass in the opening.

DANAE: "Hold the glass and don't move."

The crowd's volume increased.

CROWD: "Blooooow-job, Bloow-job!"

Danae put her hands behind her back and put her lips around the shot as if it were a dick. She bobbed slowly back and forth with her mouth wrapped around the shot glass. Next, with the shot glass still in her mouth, she tilted her head back and swallowed the shot.

Danae zipped my pants back up. Next, she stood up and took a bow. When Danae did her blow job shot, it sent me into the cookie monster mindset: *C is for cookie and cookie is for me*! If Rico knew what was going on, he would do like a gymnast and flip.

As the night matured, Danae got more flirtatious with me.

DANAE: "What are you doing after the party?"
ME: "Going back home."
DANAE: "Is that where the after party is?"
ME: "It can be. Are you trying to host?"
DANEA: "You let me know when you're ready to leave."

ME: "How about now?"

Cookies are best when they are hot and Danea was no different. She eagerly jumped in my car and we headed over to my house. During the ride over, she grabbed my hand and put it between her legs so I was feeling her sugar cookie.

DANEA: "Here's a preview of the after party."

We got out of the car, and Danea stumbled up to my room. On the way to my room, Rico and I had a brief text message correspondence.

RICO: *Great seeing you tonight. We definitely need to catch up soon.*
ME: *It was nice seeing you too.*
RICO: *Yeah let's get up on some bitches. I'm sure that slut Danea is somewhere getting fucked.*
ME: *I'm sure she is, or at least is about to.*
RICO: *Bitches ain't shit.*

Meanwhile, Danea was sprawled out over my bed. She had slipped her jeans off so that she was wearing her panties.

DANEA: "Are you going to keep texting or are you going to come play with me?"
ME: "I had to see if my friend got home alright. I'm ready to play!"
DANEA: "Well let's get this party started."

Danea was ready, willing, and able to get pounded. She pulled off her panties and bent over at the edge of my bed. With a total disregard for Rico, I went deeper into the cookie monster phase: *Her cookie is the most beautiful thing cookie monster ever sees! Me love cookie! Cookie is for me!*

I went in and started giving Danea my Big Bang Theory. I now knew why Rico was with her for so long. She had some great Lemon Meringue. After minutes and minutes of ins and outs, I filled her cookie with a few nuts.

Rico had hoped that some guy was going to take Danea home and sleep with her. I was the one to help facilitate Rico's wish; I sat in bed the next day thinking about Danea and Rosa.

I know what you're thinking. *I'm scandalous.* And I probably am. The cookie monster phase will do that to you. You lose any sense of morality, all in the name of the cookie. I decided to leave the cookie monster phase on my own accord. I still feel horrible for doing things while I was in the cookie monster phase.

Although sleeping with Rosa and Danea happened a long time ago, I never told Brody or Rico what happened. If you guys are reading this, I apologize for taking a bite out of y'alls cookie. I have no problems confessing my wrongs. So in the famous words of the cookie monster: *Cookie monster thief, not liar.*

Conclusion

I t's such a warm and comforting feeling to know that one of life's most serious and important human needs can provide so many comical situations. I decided to put together a collection of stories that have cracked laughs for many, and hopefully at least put a smile on your face.

Do I regret anything that's happened? No, because each situation is a learning experience for both these females and me. What do the females learn? Each of their experience is different but I think its safe to say that they all learned how to park my car in their garage.

What have I learned? That my sex life is funny. I don't need to be ashamed nor embarrassed by it. I embrace it. I don't plan for it to be this way, just like the girls who say they won't be sleeping with me, truly don't plan on sleeping with me. But in the end, they accept it. You see, that's the one thing these girls and me have in common—accepting things that are hard and still get joy out of it.

I actually hesitated to write this book because I didn't want to hurt anybody's feelings. But then it occurred to me—what is life if you can't laugh at the awkward moment of a malfunctioning pistol, or a porn star wanting to rock your world, or the cops knocking at the door after sex. Why wouldn't I share my stories to make another person smile? In any case, I hope you know that at any time you feel like your sex life is mundane, you can always read

my stories to either make you grateful for yours, or aspire to try something new.

Speaking of new, I recently met a girl that had a strong sexual fetish for my hands. Everytime we hang out she wants to touch and play with my palms. She claims she can have an orgasm from sucking on my fingers. Seriously? I can't make this stuff up. That will undoubtedly be another one of my funny sex stories...

About The Author

Wes Davidson is a former professional athlete and played for four different teams throughout his career. He has been a model for numerous American household brands. He once applied for the *Bachelor* but didn't get selected.

Wes loves women but often times, they love him more. He speaks reasonably decent French kiss.

If you have comments for the author,
please email those comments to
wesdavidson12@gmail.com

www.ingramcontent.com/pod-product-compliance
Lightning Source LLC
Chambersburg PA
CBHW072111270326
41931CB00010B/1519

* 9 780988 967519 *